The
Story of A Prison Wife

By

Christina Boivin

Copyright ©2023 by Christina Boivin

All rights reserved. No part of this publication may be reproduced or transmitted in any form or by any means, electronic or mechanical, including photocopying, recording, or any information storage and retrieval system, without permission in writing from the publisher

Table Of Content

Dedication 4
Intended Impact 6
Introduction 9
Book 1 19
    When The "L" Word Surfaced… 71
    The day we finally met….. 77
    Our First Date 91
    The Day I Became A Woman…. 98
    The Engagement 121
    The Birth Of A New Life…. 128
    The Day Our Lives Changed Forever 133
    THE AFTERMATH - Sept 9th 2005 141
    Deep Seeded Pain 150
    Thank you! 152

Dedication

First and foremost I have to give thanks to our creator Jehovah for giving me life and the courageous spirit that he gave me to be able to share my story. Second, I have to give thanks for my two young kings that God has entrusted to me while on this earth. I always say if it weren't for them, I don't know if I would have had the strength to mentally get through everything I have been able to pass through. Third, is my mom. My backbone and my rock through so many of my hardships, although she faced trials herself she always had my back the best way she could. Fourth, I have to say, my husband because without him I wouldn't have this story. It would be someone else's to tell. We've had many ups and downs through the years but out of it all we have raised two amazing young men who will continue to do great things in the society we live in. Fifth, is my grandmother, God rest her soul, she was a woman who rarely waivered. Although she had her opinions about the path I chose she accepted and loved my children as her own. Calling Jahleel her little Kukla, which means little doll in Russian.

I have to give thanks to all my friends and supporters who have come into my life and stayed to help me through the pain I endured. The friends who helped me keep food in my fridge, or gave me rides, the friends who were just simply there to come hang out and visit me to help keep a smile on my face. I love you all. Without them I wouldn't be here. This book is inspired by true events. Events that transpired in my life, some parts of my life that I wish never happened but they made me who I am today and for that I'm forever grateful.

Intended Impact

My Life story is one of hope and life lessons. Not only for myself but other men, women and families who also face incarceration to varying degrees. It can be utilized as a self-help tool on many levels for the following individuals in the following ways:

Loved Ones Of Incarcerated Individuals – Whether it be a spouse, parent, family member, child, friend, etcetera, The way in which I express, and break down both sides of the mental and emotional effects incarceration has on all sides can be useful in a person's individual journey.

Incarcerated Men and Women - As hard as we understand it is to wake up every day in a volatile environment, not being able to see your family and experience freedom which many of us take for granted daily, it's also hard on us on the outside. Sometimes it may even be more difficult than those on the inside. I can only speak for myself in terms of what I've done but I'm sure many of us do it. I incarcerated myself mentally! I lived in fear of everything and wasn't able to move forward on any front due to this mental incarceration.

Men and Women Released From Provincial or Federal Custody - Individuals who have recently been released from custody can benefit greatly from this trilogy. Whether you were released to society or a halfway house, my story can assist in some self discovery elements there and truly gain both perspectives of what it's like trying to reintegrate for both sides of the equation.

Parole Officers/ Correctional Officers/ Police Officers -
I'm not saying all individuals in these positions are unable to place themselves in our positions but there have been more times than not where I've personally felt there was a serious lack of understanding and compassion given to me and my family in situations that I faced. What we need more than anything is real support. It's extremely hard dealing with the traumas associated with incarceration and the fight we must battle everyday, but then when you have individuals

who have been placed in positions who are supposed to alleviate some of those stressors and do the opposite to make it harder, the effects are 10 times worse. They can cause serious short term and long-term mental health effects on all individuals in the equation.

Community Organizations That Cater To Incarcerated Individuals and Their Families –

Lived experience is the best teacher. As unfortunate as these experiences may be, they had to happen to evoke change. Many community groups can utilize my story, even reach out to me to seek advice in order to better equip the clientele that they aim to assist in these situations. I aimed to be as open and transparent as possible on this journey in order to give the reader an authentic 1st person experience through my eyes.

Introduction

You're a what? What is that? Are you crazy? Why would you be with someone in prison? Are just a few of the questions I've received over the many years since coming out publicly about my truth, my story.

As you can imagine, when people read or hear the title, "The Story Of A Prison Wife," It spikes endless curiosity in many minds. We tend to hear a lot about the negative side of prison and the men and women who are incarcerated. Most are extremely biased and demonizing point of views. Topics on prison politics, prison reform, injustice within the system, and sentencing are most common. Very rarely do we hear of the positive aspects of those who were able to take such a negative circumstance, endure through it, and turn it into something beautiful. "A Rose That Grew From Concrete", is how I like to view my life. Gotta love Tupac (God Rest His Soul) for that statement right there. The crazy thing is, I'm not even in full bloom yet. So, let me get into it. I guess the first question should be Who am I? Well, let me formally introduce myself. My name is Chrissy, and I am a strong woman, a mom to two amazing sons, who are now 17 and 13. I've successfully raised them with their dad being in prison the entire time. I'm an aspiring Author/Writer. I'm an entrepreneur who wears many hats. I'm a 'behind the scenes' community/prison supporter, as I've never been one who likes the limelight. I've graduated high school and post secondary school. And, I've been living this prison life since I was 15 years old. I'm 38 now so you do the math. Yeah, I have over 2 decades under my belt. I was introduced to Prison Life through a friend of mine who had an older brother that was locked up. You know how the story goes, big bro was looking for some girls for him to talk to and well, I was open to it. Through that connection I met my husband and my sons' father. But we'll get into all that later. I want to go into the real backstory of it all. I was a suburban young naive white girl who at that time never knew what she was getting herself into. Sure I had friends who were kind of into the street life but nothing like what I was about to experience later in my teenage years. "What were you thinking?" is a question I hear way too often. Family and friends were puzzled. I know exactly where my curiosity into that life came from though. It was my Uncle P. See, my dad was the eldest of 4 brothers. He worked hard all his life until he incurred a severe back injury at work. He then turned to alcohol and became really abusive. Reasoning as an adult now, I know he was battling depression and used that substance to try to numb his pain and escape the reality of life like many of us do. The man worked his whole life and to suddenly be told you can't work anymore would be a blow to any man's pride and ego, especially one who's prime instinct is to provide for his family. My mom now, she worked almost everyday up until her retirement. She didn't play around when it came to her providing. She knew she had to pick up the pieces. She also became an alcoholic, but again, as I reasoned, like an adult, she was just trying to survive her own demons and depression. She knew she had to be the glue that held it all together and did a great job at keeping a roof over our head. She was and is still to this day a very strong willed woman and I owe so much of my successes to her. Let's get back to my Uncle P. So he was one of four brothers and the only one who always got into trouble with the law. Arrested as early as 13 years old and that was back in the 50's. Him and my dad always got into it as kids. I used to hear all kinds of stories about Uncle P. Things he did when he was young, the fights, the jail time, the pen time, the lifestyle, his impulsiveness, etc. Every time he'd get released from doing time he'd always make his way over to our house and spend a couple of days. Every time he came through that door he was always dressed to impress. Like someone you'd see out of the *Godfather* movie. Decked out in gold, a fresh pressed suit, Shiny leather loafers, the most expensive smelling cologne, fresh haircut slicked back, and clean-shaven. He'd always walk with his black and gold comb and randomly comb his hair back. He had to make sure not one hair was out of place. Uncle P was fly! When he walked into a room, he made a statement. I remember he lived with us for a bit at one point in time because my parents had to post his bail for some alleged assault. Knowing him it probably wasn't alleged. Lol. Uncle P was a no nonsense type of man and would knock you out for the littlest disrespect. I became very into him and his lifestyle specifically because of the way he treated me when he came around. Always calling me beautiful, and his little princess. Sending me cards with money from jail reminding me how beautiful I was, how special I was, and how much he loved me. He gave me everything I needed that I wasn't receiving from my own home. See, my parents, although they were present physically, were not present with me mentally and emotionally. I was neglected in that aspect. To be very honest, I cannot remember my mom or dad telling me they loved me. Like I knew they did, but they never expressed it. Knowing that, Uncle P always went above and beyond to show me love. I felt it from him. I felt so loved and appreciated every time he stepped through that door. There was a time that set it all in stone for me. My Uncle P and my dad were sitting in the living room, talking, drinking beers, and watching T.V. I came in to ask for something, I can't remember what it was but I remember Uncle P said, "there's my darling niece," I smiled and asked my dad the question. I remember my dad being annoyed that I interrupted their conversation and he called me stupid. Who told him to do that? My Uncle P calmly put down his beer, stood up, loosened his shirt button at his neck and draped up my dad. He told him never to talk to me like that again, that I was a princess and I should be treated as nothing less. That day I witnessed that other side of him. Not only that loving caring positive affirmations side, but now a protector who would always go to bat for me, even against my dad, his own brother. He made me feel safe. So I think it's safe to assume that at that moment in time I became very intrigued by a person who lived that lifestyle. All the negative stories and judgments I had been force fed about him no longer existed. We really fail to realize how impressionable children really are. All it takes is that one moment to change the entire trajectory of one's life, one crucial moment where we as adults didn't show up for them. This is why I made it a point to always show up for my boys, especially me raising them on my own in a mother only household. I thank

God that he gave me the strength to do so even under the most difficult and darkest circumstances. I remember my dad once asked me that same question that many have asked before. "Why someone in prison?" Had I had the self-awareness and understanding I have now, or even if my dad were alive today, I'd have the real answer. It was at that moment that my own father didn't protect me from himself. Uncle P did. His circumstances, allegations, or prison bids didn't matter. He stood up for me when I needed someone to, when my father didn't.

This is not to take away from my dad as I respect him for who he was, he wasn't a bad guy but he was depressed and I do not hold that against him. That was the defining moment in my life and where I became attracted to that lifestyle.

Fast forward to when I was 15, that's really where it all began and let me tell you, no amount of preparation could have helped me prepare for the emotional Rollercoaster ride I was about to embark on. Like I said I'm over two decades into this *Prison Life* and I've been loyal to it. I'm finally on my way to becoming free from the fears that held me back from accepting my life's choices and circumstances and I'm ready to tell my story. I'm not afraid of the stigma or judgments anymore. I'll be sharing the good, the bad, and the ugly; with nothing held back and no one's emotions spared. At the end of the day this is my story, my truth, and I give myself permission to feel it and express it as I've experienced it. I've had the pleasure of hearing Jacqueline Dixon speak. She's a strong woman and community leader that I look up to here in Toronto. And on those occasions she spoke, these words stuck with me, "Our Story Is Our Strength!" Those words right there were a confirmation that I had to speak about my struggle and my life. Not only is my story my strength, my story can be and will be an inspiration for many individuals who live this life. I hope to shed light and provide insight for my perspective in the way I perceived it. Incarceration, one way or another affects us all. I can say I have successfully raised what are now to be almost grown adults, with their father being incarcerated their entire lives! Although I've been through tough times, I am stronger for it and I wouldn't change the set of events I've experienced for the world. I am who I am because of it.

Book 1

A Story of a Prison Wife

Book 1

Overall I did grow up in an emotionally neglected environment, and witnessed my dad being abusive to my mom, and oh my mother was a hoarder as well!! Other than that I had an okay childhood for the most part. I grew up in the H section of Brampton, Ontario, Canada. For those OG's of Brampton you'll remember when we used to refer to it in sections. The H, M, P, D sections. Ah, the good old days. I played outside a lot, I had friends, I loved animals and I was very introverted, but once I got comfortable with someone I became very loving and open. My parents were not only alcoholics but smokers as well.

My father Andy was the eldest of the brothers raised in Mimico ONT. Mimico is a small part of Toronto right on Lakeshore Blvd from about Evans Avenue down to Algoma Street. It is a southwest part of Toronto and was an independent township from about 1911 to 1967 according to Wikipedia. I know Wikipedia is not a scholarly source but I have found it to be accurate the majority of the time so we're going with that. My Grandmother, grandfather, my dad and his three younger brothers lived right on Hay Avenue for many years and became well known to the area. They were French Canadian. I do have Indigenous blood on that side of the family but the story I was told was my great grandmother was taken from her home and adopted into a French Canadian home in a further attempt to kill the blood line. Geez, now that I think of it I really don't know who I am on both sides of the family. I do know one of my cousins did get his "Native" status but we lost touch with him years back. I don't know what tribe I belong to on the Indigenous side and then who my family truly was on my Belarusian side. I hope to find out one day.

So here goes the family order, My dad was Andy, the second eldest was Uncle Matt, third was uncle P, the youngest was good old Uncle Bob. For the most part, all of them were "Straight Johns." A "Straight John" or in other words a "Square" are terms used for people who live their life without breaking the law, other than Uncle P like I had mentioned. I heard he was trouble from day one. Apparently he was incarcerated at the age of thirteen for trying to stab someone. I remember my dad telling me when they were kids that Uncle P either tried to or did hit my grandmother. My dad literally put him through a wall in their house right there on Hay Ave. My dad was always the one to keep everyone in line, well everyone except for Uncle P. My dad had to stop attending school at St. Leo's Catholic School, right off of Royal York, to go to work to support the family. He was the respected one but Uncle P never had respect for anyone, including himself at that time. The story I was told was that he fell out of a tree as a child and sustained a head injury. From that point on he had never been the same. My Uncle Bob told me this one story about them playing pool in a pool hall and the fight that had resulted from it. Oh, Uncle Bob was a cold pool hustler back in the day. They'd visit different pool halls all over the city of Toronto and he'd pretend he didn't know how to play. Then once the big spenders put large sums of money up he'd clear all the balls and steal the game. Anyway, there was this one time they were discovered and Uncle P apparently had to break a few pool cues over someone's head. They went there to hustle people out of their money but yet still beat them up.

I guess you can call this a classic case of being wrong and strong.

Let me tell you about my mom now. My mom was born in Sudbury, Ontario and she was the first on that side of the family to be born in Canada to my Immigrant Grandparents. I am only a 2nd generation Canadian on my mom's side.

My grandmother or in Russian my "Babushka" was the epitome of strength for me. She was the only woman I idolized growing up. Hearing her stories of enduring poverty, starvation, *real* homelessness, survival, resilience, and triumph were so inspiring to me. That woman had such a deep appreciation for life and loved me like no other. She really loved me to my core. She felt sorry for me and the household I grew up in so she would let me sleep over and come take me to the park on days my dad was drunk. She moved from Cobourg to Toronto just to be closer to me. My most fondest life memories were with her.

She was such a light even though she had been through so much. It's always those who endure the hardest of life's trials that are always the kindest. Surviving WWII, losing family members to the war, having to lose everything when

Stalin came into power. My grandmother was born in Belarus and as I've heard we came from a very prominent family line. The story told was when coming to Canada, my grandmother and her brother had to shed their true identity to survive. My Babushka was very secretive when it came to the truth behind who she really was. Her name was not really Maria. She and her Brother Uncle Jack changed their whole identity along with my moms' dad before they came here. Yes, they had forged documents but I guess they had to do what they had to do back then. I mean we're talking about escaping a *World War* here! I mean it was one of the many most gruesome events that has occurred in history.

I've asked her so many times, I wanted to know the truth and she said it wasn't safe. I know we were related to one of the Russian Tsars. Which one? I have no clue but her family had wealth. I often wonder if it really wasn't or isn't safe or if she was just acting in fear of what she had been through. I remember her telling me what she used to see in the streets while attempting to escape. Dead rotting bodies piled up on top of one another like a fish market. There were beheaded babies and children all over the place. I mean I couldn't imagine having to survive through any of the world wars or attempted genocides. I'd break down, but I guess when you're in survival mode you just have to survive. Anyway they were able to escape and go to a series of other countries before finally arriving in Windsor Canada by Steam Ship. She told me even though she struggled for years after coming to Canada, sleeping in barns with livestock, having to cover up in hay to keep warm, she never went hungry. While working for a farm in Windsor, she and my grandfather were eating. She pointed out that there were maggots floating in the soup they were served by the farm owners. Her husband nudged her with his elbow, told her in Russian, to shut up, push them out of the way and just eat it. So she did. We think we know what hardship is when we really don't. They slowly learned English, saved money and were able to get support. They later moved to Sudbury Ontario where my Grandfather worked in the mines. They had a little house, my mom was born later in 1952. My grandmother told me everything was okay until she was born. My mom's dad, my grandfather, started drinking to numb what he had experienced during the war and would abuse both my grandmother and my mom even as a baby. I was told that she'd be sleeping in the crib and he'd come home in a drunken rage and beat her while she was sleeping. That's really sick. No amount of trauma, PTSD and mental issues can excuse that, I'm sorry. His life in Canada was however short lived. I was told he was pushed off of a chimney stack and fell to his immediate death when my mom was only 3 years old. My grandmother was left to fend for herself and survive again, only now with a small child. Back then women were not earners. She moved in with her brother and his wife and had to go to work. Her and my Aunt Helena would take turns babysitting one anothers children while at work. Years passed and she got remarried to her second husband. This time he would prove to be worse than her first husband. She told me he was so nice in the beginning. He was a Ukrainian man with a good unionized job. They bought a house together and moved to Cobourg, where my mom's little brother was conceived. It was shortly after that the real horror started. My mom's stepfather started showing sexual interest in my mom when she was just 9. He would try to see her naked in the bath and touch her inappropriately with a towel. My grandmother never thought anything of it because she wasn't in tune with that type of abuse. He raped her at 11 and continued to do so up until she was around 13 years old. Sometimes he'd rape her with a gun right beside the bed as intimidation. She never knew what sex was until she turned 13 and a friend of hers told her. That's when she started threatening him and said she would tell on him if he tried to touch her again. He then threatened to kill my grandmother if she even thought of saying anything. There were a few attempts on her life to show my mom that he wasn't playing around. Gramma was taking a bath and he came into the bathroom with a wet pillow and covered her head with it in an attempt to drown her. Thankfully, although very tiny, she was able to fight herself free. My mom left home very early. He even went as far as murdering her pets to show her what could happen. Can you imagine what type of fear and trauma that caused? This is why I place no blame on her for who she became later on in life. At the age of just 18 she picked up and moved to Toronto. She enrolled in Police Foundations at Seneca College but never made it through. She said she couldn't handle seeing dead bodies. Mom had always had a soft stomach for those things. She'd gag over the smallest of things. Her grandmother came over to visit from Russia one day and it was then that she discovered that my mom had been "interfered with" as they put it. She had watched the behavior of my grandfather around my mom and asked my grandmother one day, "when did he interfere with her?" My grandmother was confused because she hadn't known anything like that had happened. She wasn't paying attention.

Her own mother, being in the country for just a few days, caught it immediately. When my mom showed up they all sat down and spoke. The question was asked and my mom admitted that yes she had been violated for many years as a child. Of course my grandmother went into shock. I don't think she'd ever forgiven herself for not seeing the signs. She immediately left him and filed for divorce. She did go to the police but they didn't believe her so he was never criminally charged. A few years later he ended up dying of a heart attack on the hallway floor of his house. My mom's little brother was the one who found him. I can't imagine how hard that was for him.

But, let's get back to business here and briefly go into how my mom and dad met. The pair met in Mimico in some bar. My mom was 20 and my dad was 33. They were thirteen years apart, sheesh. Age ain't nothing but a number so they say, and they fell in love. They got married only 6 months into their relationship and moved in together. My mom got a job as a Customs Officer and my dad was a lead hand at Red Star Express. He was part of the *Teamsters Union*.

My parents tried to conceive for many years, over a decade and many miscarriages later, at the age of 32, mom got news she was pregnant with me. I was born in St Joseph's Hospital off of the Queensway in Toronto and stayed on Superior Avenue at the time. We lived in Mimico for about 4 years before we moved to Brampton. The funny thing is I have no memories of that time other than with my grandmother, not one. You'd think I'd be able to remember something at the age of 4 from my home life but I don't. I also realize, into my adult life, there are situations that people remember vividly that I also should be able to recollect. Because I was there as well but I have no recollection of those moments. It's so strange. I guess, as I get further into my healing journey I'll learn more about why I experienced that and maybe even uncover some of those memories.

We moved to Brampton when I was 4 and I attended Hilldale Public School. I still remember all of my teachers. I'm not going to mention their names for privacy reasons but I loved them all, from JK straight to Grade 5. When I got to Williams Parkway, that's when I started having issues with teachers. I also started acting out, smoking, etc.

That is where all my real memories started, Habitat Square. I remember my friends, family life, school, playing outside, making mud pies in the backyard, Uncle P coming over, etc. That's where I really remember Uncle P coming around a lot. Uncle P was a very strong and handsome man. Don't get it twisted, I wasn't infatuated in that way, I just noticed that he always looked very well put together and had a swag about him. Confidence personified. It looked like he was doing well. He always had this cool and calm attitude when he was around us. He also made it quite clear that he would "deal" with anyone who messed with him or his family. I didn't know exactly what that meant at the time but I assume now as an adult; that he would give the person a beat down or something along those lines. I would say his energy sucked me right in. He made me feel protected, safe, and untouchable. He would always tell me that I was his favorite niece and he would never let anyone hurt me. He would always take care of me. I definitely felt special seeing as he didn't even go and visit his own children but he cared so much for me. When my dad turned into Mr. Hyde, Uncle P had me.

Pops was super depressed and that's why he drank so much. He was diagnosed with degenerative disc disease, slipped discs, herniation, and Parkinson's disease. He shook a lot. He was a man who always worked and when it came to the point where he couldn't work anymore, he fell into a deep depression. And with the depression and a lack of faith and strength in God he turned to alcohol as his savior. He drank excessively and when he did, he would call me all sorts of hurtful names. He'd say I was fat, chunky, ugly, lazy, good for nothing, etc. He would throw things at me and yell for no reason. That was the depression speaking, but as a child I was devastated when he said those things to me. With Uncle P it was different, he defended me and put my dad in his place when he said those things to me. He always took me aside and told me I was a beautiful young girl and not to let assholes get me down. I was five years old and yes he did swear. That's exactly how he said it too. He never sugar coated anything, he was who he was and if you didn't like it he'd tell you to leave and if you didn't leave his presence, he'd make you leave. I knew from young he was involved in some sort of organized crime but I don't think he was high up in rank. My uncle Bob, who is the baby of the brothers, still tells me stories about all the Italian families that uncle P had dealings with; all the way to families in New York. I never took too much interest in all that though because it's not something I was ever interested in. The past is the past. It all makes sense now that I look back at it as an adult though. He was my protection whenever he came over. How could a little five-year-old girl not feel loved and protected in such circumstances? Even though he was a criminal, I viewed him as my protector, my hero in times of need. Fathers are the ones that are supposed to be there to protect their daughters, though I never felt that way. My dad was so embarrassed about his shaking he would barely come out of the house. I was in Grade 1 when I had my tonsils and adenoids removed, so that would make me about 6 years old at the time. You know my dad never came to the hospital once? Not once. I was there for a few days and it was just my mom that was there with me. I remember there was this young girl in the bed beside me and she was having a really hard time healing from her tonsil surgery. I had a little mermaid coloring book so I coloured her a page or two to make her feel better and gave it to her before I left. I think it was then I realized I was an empath but I didn't know exactly what it was. I remember feeling like I was the one hurting and wanting to take her pain. Anyway back to my Pops.

I'd watch him sit in front of the T.V. downing beer after beer until he passed out on the couch. I loved him, yet I was afraid of him and in the same sense I pitied him. I remember standing by the kitchen/dining room entrance watching him nod off on the couch. He was so drunk at times that he would fall asleep with the cigarette still lit in his hand! We had this amazing navy blue shag carpet and all around the areas where he sat and drank there were black burn marks everywhere. I really don't know how that house didn't burn down. Sometimes it would catch fire but thank God I was there when these things happened. I would pick the cigarettes off the floor, put them out and pour water on the carpet to make sure it didn't burn anymore. The amount of times I saved that man I swear. He also had issues with stomach ulcers and there was a time where I was about 13 or 14 year old where my dad almost died in front of me. He was shitting and vomiting blood but yet still didn't go to the hospital. So, I stayed up all night on one living room couch while he slept on the other. Oh yeah him and my mom didn't sleep in the same bed either. When I was young, I slept in my moms room with my mom and Pops slept on the couch. I can't recall one day where he slept upstairs. That's really weird now that I think of it.

A Story of a Prison Wife

You're now probably asking yourself, "where was her mother"? Well, my mom is always working. I did at one point have babysitters from Ukraine or Russia, they'd come live in but I was told that they even feared my dad when he was drinking. So, they never stayed long. I also learned to speak a little Russian and Ukrainian when they were there because they couldn't speak English at all. Maybe my mom couldn't afford to have them anymore because I do remember cigarettes, alcohol, and pet food took most of the money. I always felt like I wasn't important enough for them to stop the bad habits. So my mom worked all day, my dad was home all day drinking. But one thing he did do, was walk me to school and walk me home for lunch. My lunch times were great memories for me. Some days I ate Kraft Dinner, soup, beiners and weans. That is beans and hotdogs for all who don't know. My dad could make a mean stew. I used to love his stews. I'd sit in the living room, eat my lunch while he was of course drinking a beer, watch Leave It To Beaver, *The Andy Griffith Show*, *Bewitched*, *I Dream of Jeanie*, whichever one of those shows were on at the time. Til' this day I still feel such nostalgia when I watch those shows. Especially the old Christmas shows like the original clay Rudolph, or White Christmas. I did grow up watching those movies with my parents. They were really into watching T.V. Television was life in our house. My dad was actually really awesome when he wasn't drinking. He had a great sense of humor and he wasn't abusive. Those are the rare days I miss.

As time went on I started to get fat when I was around 7 going on 8 years old. We didn't have properly balanced diets and I was eating a lot of unhealthy stuff. My mom would work all day and be too tired to come home and cook. So take out and fast foods it was for the most part. At 7, I started cooking my own breakfasts on the stove and eating whatever I could, because my parents were too hungover some mornings. I don't blame my mom though. She was so depressed and she drank to numb the pain. I also fell victim to alcoholism but we'll get into all that later in the story. I literally started down the same path I said I would never travel down. My dad was earning an income but it was CPP disability and compensation for his injury. I think at the time the mortgage percentage rate was 11% so my mom worked her ass off. She was depressed because of my dad. His behavior toward her and I when he was drinking, the fact that she was the main earner in the house, but also because she had a really hard life herself and hadn't dealt with the trauma she endured in her life. Unfortunately, these are life situations that many of us or our loved ones have faced that have caused depression and unhealthy substance abuse problems. It's only within the last 10 years I'd say that mental health has really become a forefront topic.

My mother's virginity was taken from her when she was just 11 by her brother's father. She was raped over and over again. A few more men also raped her after that. Statistics say that women or children who have been raped or molested are seven times more likely to be raped again and that's exactly what happened.

My mom tried to be a good mom but couldn't see that she wasn't being the best she could because of the alcohol she drank to numb her feelings of the past. My mother also started to compulsively hoard which really affected me negatively. According to an article from the psychiatric times, children of hoarders progressively become mentally ill in certain aspects of life. Post Traumatic Stress Disorder, Anxiety, OCD, Depression, and Social Isolation disorders are all long term symptoms of parental hoarding disorders. I also became a bit of a hoarder at one point during my childhood. My mom didn't just hoard things that were collectable, she hoarded everything from garbage, old food, old clothes, furniture, kitchen utensils, and animals, basically whatever you can think of, she hoarded. There was cat and dog feces all over the house. It wasn't too bad when I was really young; I still remember there being room for me to walk but as I got older it got worse. The animal hair clumped into what used to be the amazing blue shag carpet that I previously rolled and took naps on while the sun gleams in from the backyard door. I started not wanting my feet to touch the floors anymore because they became sticky with dog and cat urine. I noticed instead of my mom cleaning it up she'd start putting paper towels over the mess and leave it there for weeks. This is where it started to get really bad. Downstairs was so disgusting that I would just stay upstairs and watch T.V. all the time. My parents never spent time with me; they never really sat down and conversed with me, did homework, nothing. I was always alone, playing in the basement or outside. As an adult, I can honestly say I was so neglected and unloved. I remember the police coming to my door one day because my dad beat my mom. There was swearing, fighting, beer bottles being thrown, etc. At one point my parents separated. I don't remember this clearly. But my mom was leaving my dad for another man by whom she got pregnant while they were separated. Now that I'm really digging deep, my childhood was a little off and no one ever knew, and if they knew they didn't care. I loved escaping to my grandmother's house in Toronto because either she or my Uncle would play with me. They would take me places to have fun. It was my escape. She also came frequently to our house in Brampton to just take me to the park down the street. She didn't like my dad at all and knew he was an alcoholic and, because of what she had experienced with my mom, she was afraid that something would happen to me. On one hand I had my grandmother who made me feel safe, and then on the complete opposite I had my Uncle P. Even though he did over 20 years of his life in prison he always made me feel safe. So, at this point I thought that with all the negativities of this lifestyle came security, love, financial stability, power, respect, etc.

So, I continued to grow up in a home where I felt abandoned. I started to become really withdrawn in school. I didn't do homework and I became this really insecure and scared little girl. I was social but I wasn't, an introvert yet an extrovert in the same breath. One example, from grade one straight to grade twelve; I had never presented a project in front of the class. I had no confidence or courage because no one ever invested the time to raise a confident strong young woman. I was ignored. This experience has made me a better person today. Even though I live with the effects it caused, I'm able to love to spend time with my boys, cook and feed my family good healthy meals, I love to travel with them and enjoy their presence. I went through school just making it by. I was very smart but I was too scared to showcase it so I managed to keep myself under the radar. In my early teens Uncle P stopped coming around. I guess he was in prison again for something he had done, not too sure. Or he was on drugs. I heard he couldn't face his demons anymore so he got into opiate-based drugs. I was feeling unloved at home so I started seeking a crowd to fit into. I started stealing cigarettes and alcohol from my parents to smoke and drank with friends. I started to smoke weed, and even got some of my friends to try it for the first time. I became a little bit of a bad influence on my friends at that point. I didn't do other drugs though and I was a virgin and remained that way until just months before my 19th birthday. I started becoming attracted to certain ways of life because I felt at home. People of West

A Story of a Prison Wife

Indian backgrounds were those who accepted me and treated me like family. Plus I love the culture and the music.

My parents never cared what time I went to bed, they didn't care what I watched on T.V. in my own room. I usually stayed in my mom's room because she had a cable box in here. You know those Friday and Saturday nights when soft porn came on the movie channels? Yeah I was watching all of that. Before the cable box it was the squiggly porn and if you got lucky you'd catch a little action but you could always hear it clearly. Don't get uncomfortable now; you know most of us did it! I used to record some on blank VHS tapes and hide them in the back of this huge filing cabinet we had full of tapes. I'd label them cartoons so no one would suspect it. Not like they would even notice anyway. I mean I stole full cigarettes out of their packs, took the large and halved butts out of their ashtrays while they were home! Eventually I started stealing full packs out of the freezer. I wouldn't do that too often though because they would definitely notice. I remember my mom cussing out my dad about smoking so much. It was never him, it was me the whole time. I never fessed up to it even after I told my mom I was smoking. Eventually I started buying my own packs from the Chinese restaurant at the Bramalea City Centre. I had always been taller and fuller bodied than a lot of my peers so no one really questioned my age or me. Anytime they'd ask for my ID, I'd say it was in the mail and I'm still waiting for it to arrive. What the hell kind of lie was that? Like how did I even think that would even be believable? I knew they didn't believe me but they had to ask for formality or legal procedure I guess. They just wanted to make sales and I don't blame them. Shoot, I was a teenager who smoked and wanted to buy cigarettes; if it weren't from them, I would just go buy it from somewhere else. Anyway, that's enough of that. Let's now fast forward to my teenage years. I'm in high school, at this point, North Park Secondary School to be exact. And that Ladies and Gents is where I really started to backslide. I wasn't a bad kid, I wasn't having sex or anything, remember I held onto my virginity until just a few months shy of my 19th birthday which I'm super proud of but like I said I did drink alcohol, I was smoking weed and cigarettes. I also started skipping classes in and around grade ten. I think the worst thing I did in school was smoke weed and cigarettes in the school bathrooms on washroom breaks and go back to class higher than a kite.

I remember this one day like it was yesterday. I was in history class; I wish I could remember my teacher's name. She was a short older woman, very nice, but…. It was an extremely boring class. I really had no interest in history at that point of time in my life. To be very honest, I don't even know how I even passed that class. I must have gotten a 65% or something even though I probably deserved a fail because I made no effort. But I always did well on my exams. I'd retain information but wouldn't submit homework or projects. I was really just in a state of existence. If I just applied myself I would have easily achieved honors. I've always been academically inclined and I learn very quickly, especially when I pay attention. Math and English were my strongest subjects. I even received an award and a whopping $75 check from the school for getting the highest mark in grade 11 Math and I wasn't even trying.

Let's get into the nitty-gritty of how I really got into this

"PRISON WIFE" life.

I had a girlfriend who moved from our side of Brampton and transferred to Heart Lake Secondary School. She made new friends whom I was introduced to, as we were still very close. This was grade 10 I believe. I met...... let's call him Kevin so we don't call any real government names here. I met him through her then boyfriend... let's call him Junior and Junior best friend E. (God rest his soul as he lost his life to gun violence just a couple years ago) E was a great friend. Always calling to check up on everyone, fun loving, and devout Christian at the time. I was shocked when I heard the news of his passing. All of us were. Especially the way it went down.

They all went to the same school. As Kevin and I became closer friends I learned that he had an older brother who was incarcerated and facing trial on a second-degree murder charge. His name was.... Let's call him Thomas. I think I was about 15 years old at this point. I remember the day I met him so clearly. Well, the first day we spoke, not met, I was in my room bumping Aaliyah *One In A Million* on my silver with blue highlight Kenwood boombox with detachable speakers. The phone rang, I looked over and it was Kevin's number that showed up on the call display so of course I answered. I always commandeered the cordless phone, I was such a phone bug. I answered and it wasn't just Kevin on the line. He three-wayed with his big brother Thomas. We all spoke for about 15 minutes or so before Thomas asked if he could have my number and call me directly. I was like sure, of course, why not! Ha Ha, no I did not say it like that but I did say okay. He immediately collect-called me within minutes of him getting off the phone with his little bro. This was the first collect-call I had ever received. That collect call was the beginning of never ending high phone bills, canceled lines, collections calls etc. Man, if I only had the same knowledge then that I have now. It's okay though, as one of my favourite rappers Mechanic T.I.D. would say, "we don't take it as losses, we learn lessons!".

The phone rang, and Bell Canada showed up on the caller display. I answered quickly as I didn't want to chance my dad picking up the phone and hearing a collect call. I hear, "This is Bell Canada, You have a collect call from…. I heard his voice as he said his alias name….. press 1 to accept this call or press 2 to refuse." I had a little bit of a heart flutter at that moment but I said 'Here we go', I pressed 1. The Bell lady said "Thank You For Using Bell Canada." It's crazy because at no point did I ever consider I would have to pay for these calls. I don't know what the hell I was thinking. Well, the call was accepted, and boom, there he was, the first person in jail that

I developed a friendship with. Now, just to be clear, this is not the man I had children with or married. We actually never met in person. I met my husband through him but we'll also get into all that later on in the story. It's kind of messed up but I'll break down my whole process and what I went through as we get there. So, he's there, on the line. I'm of course behaving really shy although I'm a great conversationalist. I didn't know what to say at all to be very honest, so at that moment I was hoping he'd carry the conversation. We started off by the regular small talk like how are you, how old are you, what are your interests etc. I lied and told him I was 16 instead of my real age of 15. I don't know what an extra year would do in this case but whatever, I was 16 and I was sticking to it. He told me he was 18, which would have made us 2 years apart. Well, Later on down the road I found out he was actually 20 years old. That's a five year age gap and as an adult that gap isn't so bad but when you're 15, reasoning as an adult now, that's not right at all. But see when you're in the moment you don't really think of these things. I was also very mature for my age so I could pass for older. My parents had me when they were middle aged and older. My mom was 33 and my dad was 46 when I was born so I had always reasoned far beyond my years. I am what you'd call an old soul. I grew up on black and white movies, westerns, and 50's Rock n' Roll and Mo-Town. I'm a die-hard oldies fan to this day. Don't play with my oldies. I can even go as far back as Bing Crosby and The Andrew Sisters if you think I'm playing. So let's get back to that phone call. He did carry the conversation for the most part. He ended up calling back a couple times. I ended up learning a little about his background, his charges and his upcoming transfer. He had been recently sentenced and awaiting transfer to the federal system aka the Penitentiary or the Pen. He was the eldest of three that were charged in a shooting in Toronto. I think it was the first of many cases where people started getting the "guilty by association" thrown at them and where they bumped youths up to adult court to make an example of them. They were what you would call co-accused.

<u>Noun. co-accused (plural coaccuseds) (law)</u> **<u>One of two or more people accused of the same offence</u>**.

Over time we started to develop a relationship. My feelings started to grow deep. I've never had anyone pay attention to me like this before. We spoke everyday, he taught me things and expanded my mind. Him and I were both

Geminis so we had a lot of similar characteristics and personality traits in common. I was starting to fall for him hard. I think I became his girl at some point because we were acting as if we were in a committed relationship although we never met.

After a few months of us talking, some people started coming out of the woodworks saying certain things and making accusations. People started coming to me saying that they were aware of him having relationships with other women. Of course this would be the case because why would he ever take a teenager seriously even though I was and still am a very serious person, especially when it comes to my relationships across the board. I don't play about mine! One of the people who approached me about knowledge over another woman was one of my friends. Let's name her...... Savi. She was friends with another girl from a different high school that was just down the street. This day I also remember very vividly. It seems like I remember all the negative stuff vividly. I wonder why? I'll have to delve into that later too as part of my healing process and understanding my psychology.

Anyway, I was sitting in grade ten science class one day; Mr. Arms was our teacher. He was such an amazing teacher, probably one of my favourites out of my entire five year high-school stay. Yes, I said five years, that is correct, I stayed back for OAC because I was slacking and needed extra credits. I took careers and civics repeatedly and failed every time. It's not like I didn't understand, it was just so boring that I couldn't get my head in the game and do the work. Funny enough, when I actually focused in ILC (Independent Learning Center) I got a 96% in both courses and I really had to give my head a shake in disappointment. If only I focused and got it over with the first time around. I still have these strange dreams til' this day about failing my high school classes. I guess subconsciously that still bothers me. Let's get back to the story though, I'm getting a little off topic. So, my girl comes into the class and sits down at her desk right in front of me. She opens her binder and gets her pen out etcetera and then turns around and stares at me with this weird look on her face. She's like, "Ugh, I have something to ask you." I responded, "okay" and I laughed a little because she was acting so awkward. She asks, "You're talking to Thomas right?" I answered, "Yes." She proceeds to ask me, "Kevin is his brother right?" and "Kevin goes to Heart Lake right?" I'm like, "yeah why?" She tells me "her girl .... just told her about some guy she just started talking to and it's the same person."

So of course I'm shocked at this point because not only had I never been cheated on but also this was the first time I had a boyfriend/love interest or anything of that sort. Whether it was on the outside or inside I still considered what we had as a relationship. Was it really cheating even though there was no physical contact? I know I felt as if I was being betrayed and cheated on, even if it just was in the emotional aspect. My heart sunk into the pit of my stomach. I was a big girl so I struggled with my self-confidence and now this killed the little self-esteem that I had. As time went on, I found out about other women he was talking to; too many of them to count. I can't tell you how many times I cried over this man I never met, and yet I stayed because of how I felt. Wow, heart broken over a man I never met. I did have love for him and I thought he loved me too. Crazy thing is we are still friends to this day. He has since apologized for all the wrong doings and games he played with me. He said he was young and didn't quite know how to even process his emotions of being sentenced to life at such a young age and I kind of just got caught in the crossfire.

I remember this one woman someone told me about. One of my good friends from Malton told me he was messing with this older woman that just so happened to be messing with Thomas at the same time. Ronald was sleeping with her and she was carrying on a relationship with Thomas who was in prison, let's call her Jane. She would send Thomas money and would go to visit him as well. At this point he was in the penitentiary getting in person touch visits from her. I eventually became a little numb and told him I was cool with it because I couldn't see him even if I wanted to, I was still a minor and I only had a part time job. She was a grown woman who also financially supported him, paid for his phone card money, sent him canteen money, etc. At this point he knew my real age and I knew his. I didn't even find it weird. I was attached to him emotionally even though it was destroying me inside. My self-esteem was gone, and I was nothing. I was shown I was nothing from such a young age. Although I had little to no self-esteem, the one thing I was proud of myself for was being a virgin. Most of my friends around me were sexually active, they'd even engage in sexual activity in the same room I would be in. But I was never inclined to do anything with anyone. Guys tried but I knew who I was when it came to my sacredness. I knew I wanted to remain a virgin as long as I could and only give myself to the right man. One man. I valued that part of me so much that I had never given it to anyone. That person had to be worthy of receiving that part of me. Isn't that strange, horrible self-esteem yet I knew my value?

There was one day that really broke my heart into pieces and solidified everything for me.

See I had this tendency to pretend that I am okay with situations or scenarios that I'm not okay with. In an attempt to see how far those situations will carry out or how badly that person will hurt me. Most would call this self-sabotaging behavior, but I look at it as if it's unveiling behavior. We never know what a person is capable of doing unless you let them do it. If a person truly loves you they will never partake in anything that could derail you emotionally. That's just the way I saw it. Everything I shouldn't have been okay with I pretended I was. Sure, it can be looked at as misleading or manipulative on my end but what I really think I was looking for was a way out without saying I wanted out. It was like, hurt me even more so I have an excuse as to why I'm going to leave you. I knew this was bad for me, it was already killing me, but I needed to see how far he would take things with Jane. So I pretended that I was okay with Jane going to see him, taking his calls, even doing sexual things with him during the visits. I mean it's not like I would do any of those things anyway because I had never been touched before at all. Well, no sorry let me correct that. A teenage boy molested me once when I was a child but I had never done anything with anyone on my own accord. That situation is what caused me to be curious about sex and the soft porn I saw on the movie networks, but I never acted out on it. We'll just leave that right there.

Jane was providing him with money, comfort and conversation, etc. One day he calls me and tells me that Jane gave him oral sex under the table during a social visit and proceeded to tell me how good it felt. Told me he even nutted in her mouth. "Nutted" is a term for cumming or ejaculating for those who may not know. Now because I had never been sexually involved in any capacity with anyone I was so thankful she was the one doing all that. Plus the era I grew up in, we didn't suck dick anyway. Oral was looked at as very taboo in the Caribbean community when I was growing up. Things have definitely changed now. I was too young and yes, I may have lost myself in him emotionally but I would never lose myself in that way. I was, however, so heartbroken. Now he officially physically cheated. I know you must be thinking what in the world is wrong with this girl and why would she keep herself in this situation? Honestly as I write these words down, I'm thinking the same thing. That is what happens when you have a young insecure girl who was emotionally neglected, misled and mistreated from a young age. You need to instill life, belief, love, and confidence into your children. It's so imperative. I was about 16 at this time dealing with grown adult issues, prison, infidelity, etc.

I don't even know what I was thinking in those moments but I continued talking to him. I started to distance myself from him although it was hard. I was still close with his brother and his mom; even had dinner with his family at times. I was there for a lot and tried to stay busy with friends, school, work, and etcetera. I forced myself to go numb and now looking back to what I've also recently gone through, I realize me numbing is my survival instinct because I truly fear my real emotions. I've bottled them for way too long. What also helped me was that I started to take interest in someone else. Let me now get into how I met my husband and the father of my children, Lewis. I met him through Thomas. Thomas had given him my number to do some 3 way calls. Lewis was one of Thomas' co-accused. So I now started taking collect calls from Lewis as well. I would make 3 ways to his family members, his then girlfriend and friends etc. It didn't really seem like he had a lot of support from his family, which was sad. I felt really bad for him. He seemed like a really good person that just got caught up in the system, which is usually the case, isn't it? Especially when there's a young black or indigenous youth involved. The system works exactly the way it was built to work.

So, now my phone bills are skyrocketing because someone else is calling my line collect. My poor mom got mad at me every time she got the bill but she enabled it and paid it out of love for me. I can't even tell you how much my phone bills were. They started at a few hundred but I remember them going up to about over a thousand at some points. My poor mom paid them all. I appreciate her so much but she let me get away with too much, she really did. I did initially meet

Lewis when I was 15 but I didn't start the 3 ways until I was 16 years old. He was 2 years older than me and was still in a youth facility when he first called. It was called TYAC. Toronto Youth Assessment Centre I believe is what the acronym stands for. I've never been there before but I know it used to be located near Horner Avenue, which has since turned into the new Toronto South Detention Centre. I've heard it being referred to as "Guantanamo South," "a Billion Dollar Hell Hole, and Plea Factory" according to an article I read in the Toronto Star newspaper, dated Dec 13, 2019.

At the time Lewis was serving the least sentence out of his two co-accused of approximately five and a half years, give or take. I don't know the exact time he was sentenced to. Lewis was arrested at just 16 years old. Although 2 of the people involved in this case were minors, they were one of the first youth cases in Toronto to be bumped up to adult court and receive adult sentences for a crime committed when they were youth. This is very unfair and studies over time have proven that a young male's prefrontal cortex in the brain isn't matured (where it plays a pivotal role in cognitive control functions). The prefrontal cortex doesn't fully develop in a male until 25 years of age as compared to females a few years earlier than that. Girls mature before boys; I mean we all knew that right? How can you expect a child to reason as an adult and handle them in the same way you would an adult who's fully developed? It's ridiculous. But anyway, When Lewis and I had our first real conversation; I knew there was something different about him. He was super fun loving, a little goofy at times, loved to laugh and joke around, and he was very smart and had big goals and big dreams. I was always attracted to ambition, as I was quite ambitious myself. I could see and feel (even though we had never met) the genuine care he had for people in general. He's also a person who loves creating and sustaining relationships. He was so smart and driven. He was a total history buff too just like my dad. There's nothing my dad didn't know. In psychology they tend to say that women lean toward settling with partners who emulate their fathers to a certain degree. Now obviously my dad never had anything to do with prison other than the experiences with my Uncle P, but it was his knowledgeable character. He seemed like he had a strong protective nature, the provider mentality, definitely the intellectual one of the family. He was a true example of the head of a household with the ability to lead. I saw past all the B.S. all the labels that the system tends to throw on people. I saw the real him and even though I was just his friend, and he had a girlfriend at the time, I was starting to fall for him. I would find myself oddly listening in to his phone conversations with his girlfriend kind of wishing it was me. At this point I'm trying to mentally distance myself from Thomas because of all the B.S. he was on. He was just playing games with me and putting me through emotional torture anyway. I've never been the type of person to be able to cut people off no matter how badly they hurt me; I have a serious issue with abandoning people even though it may be bad for my health. I started talking to Thomas less and Lewis more. I was even writing letters at this point in between his absences when he was in further institutions. See he was actually really considerate of the phone expenses. He didn't want to be a burden on anyone so when he was at the Provincial jails out of town he wouldn't call too often. He'd call maybe once every week, two weeks or so to check in and get a three-way call. I think he and his girlfriend must have ended up breaking up because as soon as he came back to the city, he was calling regularly. At this time I was 17 and he was 19. Now I lied to him at one point and told him that Thomas and I were no longer talking but we were still in communication. I just didn't know how to tell Thomas I didn't want to be in a relationship with him anymore. He had broken me so bad it should have been an easy task but it wasn't at all. I still had love for him and still do as my friend til' this day, as I also love his mom and brother. We are still in communication twenty years later. One day I knew as my feelings grew deep for Lewis I had to tell Thomas that I was done and to stop calling. I was sitting outside in the sun on my front step by the garden hose rack. Feet planted on the driveway. I rushed home from school to make sure I didn't miss his call. I must have waited about 30 minutes for him to call. My thoughts were racing, my heart was pumping, was I making the right decision? Should I stay? Were all the questions that were arising in my head?

The phone rang and my heart sank, it was Thomas. I hesitantly accepted the call knowing what I was about to tell him. As soon as he heard my voice he knew something was wrong. I told him I had something to tell him, he already knew, he said, "you're leaving me aren't you?" I responded with a Yes. I started crying and telling him I'm so sorry but the way he treated me broke me down so much that I couldn't take it anymore. He told me he loved me and he started crying too. We sat there on the phone just sobbing with one another. Although Thomas was messing around I knew he really loved me by that day. No man would cry over a woman like that if he didn't love her. He begged and begged me not to leave and he said he'd change but I was already out. We sat there for 2 more calls after that just crying together. By the end of the third call, we knew it was over. We said our goodbyes and that was it. I was questioning myself so badly. Was I making the right decision? Was Lewis going to be any better or would Lewis just do the same thing Thomas did? Play around and cheat on me. Well, I guess that was for me to see and experience. We decided we'd continue to be friends, which we are until today. At this point Lewis and I were starting to.... I guess you would call it courting. Yes, he was courting me. He'd call everyday at lunch, and when I got home from school. We started to develop real feelings. He started opening up and telling me about his upbringing, his mother, adopted mother, his street lifestyle, etc.

The connection I had with him was something different, he was "street" but he had such a huge heart. "Street" or "Hood" are terms we use for an individual who knows the street, has credibility, or has developed a respect or a reputation in the streets normally through hustle or illicit activities. He had a hard life, way worse than mine. People in society these days don't care enough to try to understand the reason behind why youths turn to the streets to hustle. I'll let you know just a bit of what he went through as a young baby to teen hood.

See, his mom committed suicide when he was just a baby. She drank weed killer/poison one day because she couldn't take the "alleged" abuse from his dad. I don't know how true that was because they've both passed away so we can only speculate based on what we've heard. She fell into such a deep depression that she just one day decided to commit suicide. She remained alive in the hospital for almost a week. We were told by her sister that she lived in such deep regret for what she had done in that moment of weakness. She recognized that her decision was going to cause her only child to be orphaned. While on her deathbed she begged her family members to take care of Lewis because she knew she was no longer going to be here. Her stomach and intestines were destroyed from the chemicals. She prayed, begged and pleaded for forgiveness. If only she could go back in time and reverse her decision. Unfortunately, It wasn't going to happen; she died a week later leaving her poor baby boy behind to survive in this cruel world all alone. Without the person who was supposed to love him most; his mother. After his moms passing, we were told his father did care for him for a short while but then also later on abandoned him at an aunt's house. He vividly remembers the car ride from home to Aunty's house that day. He expressed that this day felt different than any other. He remembers the somber feeling. He explained that as the car stopped, his father went to get him out of the back seat. He knew he was leaving him so he immediately started crying and moved to the other side of the car. His dad reached over, grabbed him and pulled him out of the car, and left him right on the driveway. He bawled as his dad drove off. As he stood with his Aunty, he knew he was being abandoned for the second time. He never saw his dad again. As time passed, he started to fit in and live life with Aunty Y. Just as things seemed to normalize, Aunty Y's daughter accidentally drowned while taking a bath. Turmoil came upon his household once again. One thing led to another and his uncle whom he called dad left him with his Gramma. Well it was his other Aunty but he called her Gramma. As he turned just 4, his uncle came for him and left from Trinidad to Canada in pursuit of a better life. He started calling him Dad. That was whom he knew as his father. Uncle had it pretty rough when he came to Canada. He tried to take care of Lewis as best he could but I guess it proved to be too much for him so he dropped Lewis off at his sister's house. This was yet another case of abandonment in his life. Although his uncle would come and visit, drop him money, take him places, and spend some quality time. That didn't last long. Yet again, Uncle's visits became more infrequent. He met a woman, got married and moved 4 hours away to Windsor Ontario. Lewis was crushed and abandoned again. How many times is this now? So how many is that; fifth abandonment before the age of 7? That's traumatic.

Lewis started calling his Aunt, Mom. She eventually adopted him. He stayed with her, up until he left home due to a horrible home environment. See, his adopted mom pulled him out of school at the end of grade 8 to go work for her husband, his stepfather, who was a bricklayer. Lewis spent long grueling hours doing a grown man's job at the age of only 13. Eventually he got fed up with working for free, not going to school and he left home. He tried to get odd jobs but as a person with no permanent status here in Canada, he needed a work permit and social insurance number. He didn't possess any of these documents and there wasn't anyone around him to help him apply for any of those things as a minor. So, he eventually, as options for gaining income lessened, turned to the streets. To be very honest, do you know how many youths this happens to? This is not a stand-alone scenario, unfortunately it's quite common. Why do you think young men and women turn to certain lifestyles? Sure, few may because they actually love the thrill of street life, but trust me, the overwhelming majority would say they wish they had another way out. This is even where the saying comes into play, "desperate times call for desperate measures," A world famous quote from an ancient Greek doctor, Hippocrates. Financial Castration = Desperation = Turning To Illicit Activities (for some). The sad thing is even though I may lay out the situation clear as day for someone, they'll still say "Oh he had other options...." When you're a child you reason like a child, and when you have no adult guidance it's even more difficult. It's that simple! We're all human beings and we're all capable of anything depending on our situation and level of desperation. A single mother with 3 kids who are starving might make a decision to steal groceries, like I once had, to feed her kids. While a single woman who doesn't have children who's also facing a financial crisis might just skip a meal for the night. Dynamics play a huge part. I will be going into the details of some of the decisions I've made along the way strictly for survival. Oh and there's people who will say, there's welfare, there are services etc. Yes there are, but do you know that the amounts people receive while on those services are well below the global poverty level? Do you know how hard it was taking care of a baby while only getting $850 per month and your rent alone is $875??? And I was on maternity leave as well, barely getting by. How do you eat? How do you clothe yourself? But hey, no one really thinks about all that now do they?

Those who haven't lived it can't relate, period. I'll get into all that later. Oh my I can't wait to get into all that, even up to how some social workers degraded me, made me feel less than, and completely disregarded my mental health status and everything I had been through.

Lewis left home for good at the age of 15 years old. Bouncing from family members to friends, to acquaintances etc. He got into the drug game, started making decent money and that was it. Once you get a taste of fast money it gets addictive and you become engulfed with the lifestyle it comes with. Money, drugs, partying, and sex.

Lewis started having sexual relations very young, well, I say he was molested by an older girl but she was also under age so can we really call it molestation? I mean if you expose children to things they should never be exposed to and then leave little boys and girls alone together what can you expect? He started being active under the age of 10. I was shocked! That's crazy! As shocking as it is, this happens so often. I can't tell you how many of my childhood friends opened up to me in their adult years, sharing similar stories. It's really heartbreaking. People had the nerve to tell me I was over protective, well, that's the reason why I mothered my kids the way I did. People can say what they want to say about me but one thing they could never say is that I didn't protect my kids. My sons are soon to be 14 and 18. Both have never been exposed to anything of that nature. My eldest son who's soon to be 18 years old is still a virgin!! He wants a wife!!! I have to give thanks to God because we were able to raise them right! With the help of family, Bible studies, constant guidance and family reasoning sessions I couldn't be more proud of my two young Kings.

Well, there's a quick rundown of Lewis' history for the most part, for those of you who were wondering. There's a lot more detail to be added to the equation but this is not his story this is mine. Who knows, maybe he'll come out with his side of this story later on? I guess time will tell.

Back to our friendship now, as we spoke more often, I started to develop very strong feelings for him, almost as if I just couldn't function if I didn't talk to him. He became my best friend. He never knew I was into him though. I would always offer to hook him up with one of my friends, even though I liked him. That was very stupid of me; I don't know why I used to do that. Matter of fact I did that with every guy I had a crush on. I'd always offer to hook them up. Oh well, he never took the bait anyway so that was good. He was always telling me he's not interested. As a matter of fact he probably knew I was into him or he was into me because why wouldn't he take the hook up? Any guy would unless he's interested in someone specific right?

Here I was, 16 now, just ended my relationship with Thomas and growing feelings for Lewis. As weird as it may seem to say now that I'm grown, it felt really good to say that I had connections to some serious people inside jail, at the time I felt like I was untouchable. I was like the only one in my school in a relationship with a convict, it was empowering, and it made me feel like somebody, like I was relevant.

Again, clearly not the case but that's how I viewed it. Him and I used to talk for hours, we'd talk about our childhood, goals and dreams, life, and future. I told him that I wanted to own a club. Crazy, I actually registered my first business when I was 16. It was called *Chocolate Lounge*. I opened up a bank account and was granted a business credit card with a limit of $3000. I was under 17 with credit, what???? I started throwing parties with friends to earn extra money. I was already working at *Addition Elle* part time but I love love love music and I've always known my heart belongs there. Which brought me to starting *Pivotal*. That in itself is another book, or documentary.

Man oh man, that rectangular box on that jail wall. That thing called the payphone is the lifeline for so many people who are incarcerated, the start and end to many good and bad relationships. It's the only interaction they have with the outside world. That box was where I really developed a serious relationship with Lewis, where I met my best friend, my lover, my husband, and the father of our two boys. That box on the wall had so much significance in my life.

Even though we were still just friends, I was really starting to fall in love. I used to look forward to his calls everyday. Him and his girl broke up on their own accord, so no I didn't take him away from anyone. She couldn't do it anymore even though he was going to be released in the next two years or so. We eventually started getting closer as friends over time and eventually we spent entire phone calls just talking and laughing. I really enjoyed his conversation, like I said he was smart and had a great personality and loved to talk. And he still does (a little too much sometimes I must say!) But hey, he's a talker; he's always spitting knowledge. And I liked to listen (back then) just kidding. Anyway I remember this one day, They always had the TV in the common area of the jail on BET. Mr. Cheeks from The Lost Boys new single *Crush On You* ft. Mario Winans started playing in the background. He turned up the TV on the range and told me to put mine on BET as well. He was at the west detention at the time and that was once upon a time on Disco Rd. It has since then been demolished once they opened up the Toronto South. He came back, picked up the phone receiver and started singing the hook. "I've got a crush on you my baby, so let's put a rush on us sweet lady."

My heart started beating like it was trying to jump out my chest. My face felt so hot, I'm sure I was red like a tomato. I'm sure I was smiling ear to ear. Here's this guy with a tough gangster exterior singing love songs to me on the other end of the line. It was so cute. At that point I knew I broke through his shell and I was getting to the real him. He then says, "This is a really good song huh?"

I started to get flustered and unbelievably excited because I felt like I knew what was coming but I didn't know for sure. I said, "yeah it is." He's like, "so you know I'm feeling you right?" *OHHHH EMMMMM GEEEE!* I put my hand over the mouthpiece of the phone and started stomping my feet on the ground in excitement. I quickly gathered my composure and came back and responded, "are you?" He replied, "Yeah A lot!"

I covered the mouthpiece again and did a jig while spinning around. I came back to the phone all calm and cool. I replied to him and said, "I'm kind of feeling you too!" I threw in the "kind of" because you know us girls, we never want to let a man know we're feeling them more than they're feeling us.

He then asks the question. "You want to be my girl?" At this point I don't even know. I was so excited; I had butterflies all up everywhere, I was starting to sweat, and my breathing became really shallow. Probably shed a tear too.

And of course I said yes!!! Look at me saying it as if I was saying yes to a proposal or something. That day we were official! April 11th, 2003! I will forever remember that day as our anniversary over our wedding day.

I could hear in his voice that he was really happy as well. This man was smiling through the phone. He was smiling so hard I could see it in my mind.

We spoke for hours everyday, day after day. Week after week until over a month went by. He would send me all these cute cards with his little sketches in them. He knew I was a bigger girl and he didn't really care. He was actually attracted to big women. He use-to-use the word "buxom" to describe big, plump beautiful women. There was a card where he drew an alien man who came down to earth chasing a buxom woman like they were extremely desired. He never made me feel insecure about my weight. That was definitely a "me" problem. I guess because of the way I grew up and my parents never really instilling confidence in me I always felt I wasn't good enough. As parents we have to make sure we breathe positive affirmations into our kids. I grew up hearing parents call their kids stupid, useless, good for nothing. I only got called names when my dad was drunk but I always felt I had to prove myself to get positive reassurance.

When The "L" Word Surfaced...

I don't remember exactly when it was but it was definitely after my 18th birthday, which is May 22nd, so let's say around June I knew I really loved him. I knew he loved me too. I could feel it. But I was really starting to wonder when this guy was going to drop the "L" word. We all know what that is, of course it's LOVE!

Like I could tell at the end of some phone conversations he would pause, then I'd pause, then there would be this awkward silence. I knew he wanted to, "like just spit it out already" is where my mind was at. He was extremely hesitant for some reason. One day I mustered up the courage to just spit it out, "I LOVE YOU" came out, strong and bold. After I said it I was like shit, did I really just do that? Did I really just tell this man I love him first? Who does that? What if he doesn't say it back? What if he looks at me like I'm moving too fast? Will it push him away? Were all thoughts racing through my mind in his stunned moment of silence. It was just silent....... I'm here waiting on the other end of the phone and after what felt like a damn eternity he let out this breathy laugh and said, "Wow, I love you too!"

Lordddddd...... My heart started racing, I got butterflies not only in my stomach, literally everywhere. My pores started to raise, my face got hot and of course I started smiling ear to ear. Damn, he loved me too. Our relationship really started to excel after that.

He knew I was a virgin but I don't think he knew like I've literally done absolutely nothing sexual. I mean I was 18 years old at this point and by that time a lot of girls had at least some sexual experience. Meanwhile, here I am. I haven't even been touched below the waistline. I had only kissed a couple guys up to this point in my life. I was a really good girl. Well, I still am but you know what I mean. This one day he starts to talk about sex with me, well, really trying to engage me in phone sex. Again, something I've never done before. His voice dropped into this seductive, persuasive tone, um, it was definitely a turn on.

To be totally honest though, I completely froze. I started to think of ways I could get off the phone. I didn't want to just hang up so I started thinking of other ways I could get out of this. Should I go downstairs and pull the wall plug out to make it sound like the phone lost connection? I didn't know what to do or say. Here he is talking about all kinds of sexual stuff that I never experienced and I mean yeah, damn, it sounded great but I didn't know how or what to say back. I had never done this. Omg, I was soooo embarrassed. Tomato red face again, probably starting to buss a sweat, heart racing. Same ol', same ol'. I went silent for about a minute, I was stuck, just stuck, FROZEN. He probably thought something else at the time but what do I do out of nervousness? I started laughing sooooo hard. I was so nervous I got the giggles. And don't act like that never happened to any of you out of nervousness okay! I know it must have. He got cheesed. (Cheesed is a term for being frustrated or upset)

Lewis thought I was taking him for a joke. But the reality was I really didn't know how to feel or what to do. I was soooo awkward. Keep in mind we had still never seen one another in person. I ended up telling him I've never done anything like that before and he was in shock. He said he's never met an 18 year old virgin before either. A lot of young women my age had already had multiple partners. And to each his/her own, in no way am I judging so let me get that straight. A lot of my close friends were sexually active. I never cared. I just knew I wasn't ready and I wasn't afraid to say so. Long story short that day I think he really saw me in a different light. That was the day he really claimed me and started telling everyone he was a one-burner man (a one woman man). He got a little ahead of himself saying that because when he got out he clearly wasn't ready for the level of commitment I came with. Even his fellow peers inside told him they didn't believe it. One of his friends who is still currently our friend to this day, someone I call my brother, told him, "yeah you'll see when you touch road."

<u>Touch Road Definition</u> – (when someone get released to the public from police/ jail custody after a period of time)

He had the best intentions but we have to also remember, Lewis was very sexually active from before he went to jail at just the age of 16. Add raging young male hormones to the equation and the fact that he had been locked up for almost 5 years at this point, that was a little unrealistic expectation. I'm just being honest. Especially because I was a virgin, I definitely wasn't going to give it up to him right away, so what was he going to do? He told me he'd wait but I didn't believe him. I also wanted to be a virgin until I was 19, so who knows how long he'd really wait. I kept telling him I was convinced he was going to leave me when he gets out based on his past but he assured me he loved me and he wouldn't. This is something a lot of us women fear for some reason when it comes to incarcerated men. Why do we judge and stereotype men so harshly and not show any belief in them? That must be a very horrible feeling, knowing that the person who loves you and you love in return has no belief in you, has no trust in you, that's heartbreaking. Damn, that's really heartbreaking.

Another thing that really hung over my head was I felt he wasn't going to like my appearance and would leave me for someone better looking. We had been in a relationship for months and I had never worked up the courage to go visit him yet. I don't know what I was really running from because if he was going to leave he was going to leave. Better get it out of the way sooner than later, no? But, he finally set an ultimatum and told me I needed to come visit him. I was terrified. I didn't care about how he looked, I was just afraid he wouldn't like how I looked. Although I felt this way, now the time came for me to really face my fears. I decided that the next upcoming weekend I was going. Whatever happens, happens, I was going to see him.

The day we finally met.....

Saturday morning came, my alarm went off. My stomach was in knots; the level of nervousness was out of this world. I reluctantly got up, went to shower and got ready. Made sure I straightened my hair, made sure my makeup was on point, put on a whole black on black outfit because I thought it made me look slimmer. I took one final look at myself in the mirror before I left the house to catch the bus. I took the number fifteen to the Bramalea City Centre, then hopped on the number fourteen bus to Westwood Mall in Malton. From there I called the All Star Taxi Company, I still remember the number, (905) 602-0000. Told them I needed a taxi from Westwood Mall to One Eleven Disco Road in Rexdale. It was just up the road, about a $15 taxi ride. The taxi arrived, I got in and from there I felt like I was dreaming.

The taxi man kept talking and I'm telling you I don't think I heard one word that man was saying. I think he eventually stopped talking because I wasn't responding. I was just in a zone. I was about to see the man I told I loved and he loved me. Before I knew it, I was in front of the Toronto South Detention Centre. I pulled out a $20 bill, gave it to the driver, he returned the change, I said thanks and got out. There I stood staring at the entry doors. I wanted to run so bad, but I could hear Lewis in my head saying he would never talk to me again if I didn't get over this fear. So, I put on my big girl pants, and walked into the building. I looked around, there were wooden benches built into the walls. The room was filled with mostly women and a couple kids waiting to see their dads. Some women held up their mirrors, making sure their makeup was on point, lipstick done, hair in its place. That was going to be me starting today. I stood at the end of the line anxiously awaiting my turn. I was really hoping they would start turning people away and say visits were full, but of course that didn't happen. After some time, it was my turn. I approached the cold looking encaged brick and glass area where a woman sat in a full Correctional uniform. "What's the name of the inmate you're visiting?" I leaned into the glass hoping no one would hear me as if it were some secret that I didn't want anyone to know.

Like anybody would have cared anyway, we're all there for the same reason, weren't we? Of course, just my luck, the officer behind the glass shouts, "You need to speak louder, I can't hear you." So I raised my voice and said his name again. She typed in her computer, asked for my identification so I slipped it under the glass. The officer looked at me, looked at the ID, wrote my information down on the paper and picked up the phone and told the officer on the other end to send Lewis down, he had a visit. She slid my ID back to me and told me to sit down and wait until my name was called.

I sat down for maybe ten to fifteen minutes waiting to be called. In that time I just sat there quietly, feeling a little out of place, feeling like I wanted to walk back out and go home. But I stayed. I watched as women were called in and women came out. "Visitor for Lewis", came barreling out of the speaker in the glass. That damn near scared the life out of me because I was in this weird place where I was only hearing white noise almost, like I was in a dream. I got up, walked toward the door, grabbed the door to open it and nearly pulled my damn rotator cuff. That door was ridiculously heavy for no reason. I can imagine what I looked like struggling with that door, I probably would have laughed at myself if I had seen that. Everyone else made it look so effortless. Clearly they've been there multiple times. I walked into this corridor and then I believe the visiting room was right there. I can't remember full detail, there may have been one more locked door before I got into the room but there it was. This room with solid wooden counters about waist level, solid glass from the top of the desk to the ceiling and built in metal and wood stools on either side of the desk area. Each visiting area had these large wood privacy dividers in between each cubicle area. It was also shaped very distinctively. It was shaped like an E. Let me try to explain. As you step in, immediately to my right was a whole row of cubicles. As you keep going, there was another whole row of cubicles on the other side and immediately behind that there were another two rows with the same setup. I looked at the first available one and sat my ass down. I looked at the phone handle sitting right there on the desk, it wasn't even clean. There was caked on dirt in the corners of the glass, smudged fingerprints, some cubicles had lipstick kisses all over them. I don't know about you but I sure as hell wasn't going to be putting my lips on any dirty glass, I'm sorry. Not judging anyone here but that's just not for me. I start seeing people coming and going. There was this door that prevented them from coming into the visiting room unless the guards pressed a button. You'd see a few guys standing behind the door just waiting to come out and see their loved ones. They'd all be there peeking through the long narrow glass window in that door that separated them from us. A long loud buzz would sound and the door was pushed open. When that door closed you could feel your soul vibrate. Everything just had to be ridiculously loud, geez. The only thing I liked loud was my music. Everything else is unnecessary.

I saw guys coming in, in their bright orange jumpsuits with black velcro from the waist to the neckline. As soon as they got in there, a lot of them would open it up to show off their chiseled abdominals and swollen pectoral muscles. Their smiles were from ear to ear when they'd see their families or girlfriends. Some couples would stand there for a bit and just stare at one another for a minute before sitting down. You had the guys who'd sit down and ask their women to spin around for them, bend down a little bit so they could see their ass and a little bit more buffing through their pants. I glanced around as I was studying this whole new scene I had just entered, so it didn't look like I was being too nosey but I wanted to know what this was all about. The only way I can learn is by observing right? Or was that weird? Oh well, weird or not I stayed with my eyes rolling around that room. I saw a woman secretly show her man her breasts as he stared at her like he wanted to devour her. You could tell he was starting to get uncomfortable, if you catch my drift. As I sat there observing, I saw another group of guys waiting by the door. I wonder if Lewis was in this group. I heard the buzz, the door opened, and the guys walked in. I saw this tall, broad shouldered man come up to me and start smiling. He spoke to me through the glass and told me to stand up, Oh my GOD, I blushed so hard and shook my head no. I was not going to do what everyone else was doing. I sat there waiting for him to sit down. He didn't, He stood there smiling, opened his orange jumpsuit and looked at me seductively. He told me he worked out like crazy but I could never picture what I saw. He was RIPPED! Ripped means chiseled, he had a rock hard body. Abs so pronounced they were protruding. I think he overworked those. He had these long strong arms, with these large hands. He had strong broad shoulders and back. He was a beast of a man; a perfect sculpted body. This man was definitely not joking when he said he could lift me up, even as heavy as I was. Wow, how could someone that looked like him possibly be into someone like me?

A Story of a Prison Wife

He finally sat down and just kept smiling at me. He looked at me and told me I was beautiful. He told me he loved my long beautiful hair, my green eyes, my smile, my diastema or what you'd call the gap in between my two front teeth. I was in such shock as to how good looking this man really was, I was mind blown. Like this is who I was talking to the whole time? This was the man on the other end of the phone? Oh yeah, I had it in my head that this was definitely not going to work out long term. I was definitely not good looking enough for him. The crazy thing is I made myself believe that. I convinced myself that that was true, that he was going to cheat because of how I looked. He loved bigger women, so what the hell was my problem? I could tell he was attracted to me by the way he stared at me. I've never been looked at like that in my life. That was the first time I felt so desired. We stared at one another smiling. I was in shock, and he'd let out a breathy laugh every few minutes because he knew I found him amazingly attractive. Damn, the size of this man's hands were unbelievable. His arms, long and strong as if they were meant just for me. He could definitely wrap his arms all the way around me and then some, and his hands could definitely grab parts of me with ease. Whoa whoa, I was still a virgin at this point so let's ease up a little bit. Don't want to get too hot and heavy, well, not yet anyway.

Before we knew it, the visit was over and the receiver cut off on us. I think almost 30 minutes went by. It was supposed to be only 20, but the CO's back then were a little more lenient so they'd always give people extra time. He got up almost angry and told the guard that he wanted a double. I learned that inmates in provincial jails could get 2 – 20 minute visits per week. He hadn't used either of them so he asked to use his double with me. That made me feel kind of special because I'm sure he had other people who wanted to see him as well. I trumped them I guess. We sat and spoke for another approximately 25 minutes. In that time he asked me if I wanted to see his dick. I was like hell no! I told him if he attempted to show me I was going to look away. At no point in my life had I ever seen a penis in real life other than in porn videos and my first time wasn't about to be in a jail visiting room with other people around us. He laughed it off as my face turned red and I dismissed his offer. He didn't care anyway. He went to pull it out and I kid you not I must have shot down his ego that day because I didn't even sneak a single peek. I immediately turned my head to the side and stared at the wall until he put that thing back in his jumpsuit. He laughed and said, "shit, you really weren't joking." I responded, "nope I told you I wasn't joking. I have never seen someone's dick in person and I don't want to see yours in this scenario."

He sat there staring at me in disbelief, smiling as the receivers cut off yet again. That was it, our first visit was over. I stood up, he stood up, we smiled and stared at one another for a few minutes as the CO's were repeatedly telling Lewis his visit was done. I said bye through the glass and so did he. I watched him walk away and then I left the visiting room as well. I passed through the hallway, and out that heavy metal door out of the waiting room. I walked straight outside to the daylight and fresh air. Wow, I had just met my boyfriend of months in person and he's actually into me. I called a cab from 111 Disco Rd in Rexdale to Westwood Mall in Malton so I could catch the fourteen bus back to the Bramalea City Centre, and then the fifteen back to my house. That was the beginning of many visits. I'd try to go every weekend and we'd take up every double visit. I came so regularly that the guards sometimes gave us 2 hours in the visiting room.

Day by day we grew together. We rarely argued. At this point his friends became my friends and vice versa. I had spoken to his family but hadn't met them in person yet. They didn't seem like the most supportive family and I soon came to that realization when Lewis' immigration bail came up. See, Lewis was not and still is not a Canadian resident. Although he came to Canada from Trinidad at such a young age, his family never got his citizenship for him. So as soon as he was convicted of a crime, he was placed on a deportation order. I never even thought of what I was going to do if he got sent back to Trinidad. To be very honest I think I knew God had us because it really wasn't a fear within me. I was very calm about the situation. He was a youth when the crime was committed therefore he was eligible for bail while he awaited the decision of what's called a Pre Removal Risk

Assessment aka a PRRA (Pronounced Praw) See, at that time he never knew his family back home so he thought he had no one there. Years later we found out he was purposely being kept from his family in Trinidad, but that's all family drama and I don't do drama so we'll just leave that right there! His first bail hearing came, and was denied. His mother didn't qualify to be his surety. Although discouraged he kept his faith and prayed for his release. A few days later a woman from immigration came to visit him at the West. She let him know that Immigration was going to set his bail and release him to a halfway house in Toronto, the Keele street location to be exact. God had worked it out for him in such a way where he never even needed anyone to bail him. GOD DID! HE GOT BAIL! He called me from the range and said, "Stina, I'm getting out!"

I nearly dropped to the floor, oh my God, he's coming home! He told me the plan, he had to pack up his stuff, take the bus to the Keele Centre and check in by a certain time. I immediately called into work, told them I'm not coming in today and I needed someone to cover my shift. I called my girl Rishi and asked her to drive me down to see him in the evening. She said she was down to bring me. What was I going to wear? I wasn't a girly girl, so I threw on a pair of black pants with a grey, white and black, colour block *Akademiks* velour zip up sweater. Rishi came to pick me up and there we headed off to Toronto to see my free man. I was soo excited. Rishi asked me if I was ready. Oh my, was I ready? I was going to be able to touch him, smell him, and feel him now. A man has never hugged me with passion before. What was that going to feel like? As we approached the halfway house, Rishi pulled into this parking lot by the fire station. As I sat there in the car, looking in the mirror, making sure my makeup was on point, my cell phone in hand just anxiously listening for it to ring. The ringer went off. It was a Toronto Bell payphone number. OH MY GOD, I picked up, and it was Lewis. I told him where we were and he hung up. I saw this tall handsome man with a huge smile walking our way. I jumped out of the car and started screaming "Heyyyyyy." I walked up to him with what felt like a million butterflies fluttering throughout my entire body. I felt as if I was high. Lewis quickly ran to me, slid his long strong arms around my waist, as I reached up, wrapped my arms around his shoulders and neck, for the tightest embrace I had ever experienced in my life. He nestled his face into my neck as I did his. It's as if we were using all our senses to remember this moment of one another.

Smell, sight, touch, not taste yet though. Even though I had kissed other guys before him, I shied away from kissing him too soon. He had also never really kissed another woman before so we wanted to wait until the time was right for both of us. We unlocked out of one another's arms and just stood there smiling at one another in disbelief. Lewis, who was just a couple months shy of twenty-one years of age, was on road after five and a half years being locked up. We didn't have too much time as it was his first day. He had to be in the house for most of it until he met with his Parole Officer and got his schedule going. He was free but not completely. By law he was still under Federal Corrections supervision until his full warrant expiry which was August of that same year if I'm not mistaken. He was released around the end of January 2004. The weather was gloomy, cold and snowy but it felt like a beautiful summer's day. We were on cloud nine. That first contact visit ended so quickly, I had to rush and give him everything I had purchased for him while he was locked up. I handed over some bags with a couple pairs of jeans, tracksuits, shirts, boxers, socks etc. I didn't have any hygiene products because I knew I wanted to take him shopping for all of that. My mom was and still is a huge collector of Shoppers Drug Mart points so she wanted to be the one to buy all of that for him. Wow, thinking back, my mom was so supportive. She never judged Lewis or his circumstances. I'm so thankful for her and I know he is too. He kept asking me for the time, as he knew our time was coming to an end. We embraced one more time as we said our goodbyes, only this time it wasn't going to be for long. I had plans to come down as often as possible. He walked me to Rishi's car, opened the door for me and closed it as I got in like a real gentleman. I watched in awe as he walked off in the distance toward the Keele entrance. I put on the music and we drove home. My man was home!

A Story of a Prison Wife

Our First Date

A few days had passed and he was finally allowed to go out and spend his days freely. He had been given his schedule to do his programming and hours allowed away from the halfway house. I took the bus down one day after school to have our first date. Keele and Dundas , also known as "The Junction," is located in West Toronto and given that name because of its intersecting railway lines back in the day. It has a small neighbourhood feel to it and is full of mom and pop shops, mostly along Dundas Street. Lewis and I walked around, looking at stores to see what they had to offer. We stopped in at this restaurant style pub, I can't remember the name but it was cute inside. We sat in the booth right by the front window so we could just talk and look outside while we were there. We bought a couple drinks and enjoyed one another's company. I felt his intense stares, I knew he wanted to ravish me but he promised he would take his time with me.

A few drinks and about an hour later I could tell he was feeling a little buzzed. Lewis started to move a little closer to me, placed his hand on my leg, slowly moved in for a kiss. I pulled away like a jackass for no reason. Like I knew I wanted to kiss him, he had the sexiest lips I had ever seen and I wanted to feel them against mine.

He was shocked when I pulled away, I mean Lewis wasn't exactly the type of guy most women would reject. They would clamor at the opportunity to be with him so he was a little thrown off that I brushed off all of his advances. He seemed a little upset, almost. We sat there in silence for a minute. He looked at me and asked me how long I was going to take before I gave myself to him. I told him as long as it takes. He was not accepting that because he knew I wanted to kiss him. I know he could feel it. He slid over really close to me and leaned in again, this was it, he was putting me to the test. I smiled and I leaned into him. Before I knew it our lips locked and I must say even though he wasn't an experienced kisser he did his thing! We had a whole few-minute make out session. It was amazing; my first time experiencing passion like that. I gently pulled away from him and we both smiled at one another. That was it, where real physical passion ignited in that moment. My body was screaming all sorts of things. Lewis looked at his watch, stood up. "Damn, are we leaving already?" I said in disbelief, I was just getting started, I wanted more. But, it was time, time to head back to the halfway house.

I'd come down a few times a week and we'd spend hours together. When we were in each others' presence, no one else existed. We were in love.

I remember this one day we went to the Eaton Centre Downtown Toronto with a friend of mine and her man. That day I will never forget. We were all over one another. He'd stop and kiss me in the middle of the mall as we were walking, hold my hand, open doors for me, he really made me feel like I was something special. We even got a few, "Get a room" comments from passersby. I wanted this to be our moment for life. I don't remember anything we did other than randomly stop and make out in the mall every 10 minutes.

Weeks passed and as much as we were in the honeymoon phase we started to experience our first fights and disagreements. He also started cheating. I found out about this one girl Star he was speaking to. He called her to suck his dick. The one that really hit me hard though was his ex. Lewis promised me that he wouldn't meet up with his ex. I mean I kind of mentally prepared myself for that. Like I mentioned earlier, Lewis had a lot of sexual experience and I didn't. There were times where we were alone and things got hot and heavy. We'd be passionately kissing, caressing and touching one another on our most sensual parts but we never took it to 4th base. I wanted to stay a virgin until my 19th birthday and he knew that. He said he'd wait but clearly he was eager to have sex because there was this one time we came close and thank God it didn't work out. One we were in the Parole Officers Office that was under construction and I would have always remembered that to have been the spot where I lost it, and two, I would have bled all over the damn place. That wouldn't have been cute. Let's get back to his ex shall we? Let's call her Sarah. See, they were together at a young age but she had so much past childhood traumas that she hadn't resolved. Due to those traumas she was seeking attention in ways that weren't healthy. I don't doubt that she loved Lewis and I know he loved her but she hurt him badly. She was sleeping with a few guys from his neighbourhood and ended up getting pregnant by one of them. He told me she ghosted him and then one day randomly showed up to a visit pregnant. I'm pretty sure that was the last visit they had.

Well, he decided to call his eldest sister and ask for Sarah's number. They met up at the same bar we went to for our first date, had some food and drinks and caught up I guess. They then proceeded to the bathroom where he told her to give him head. He told me she started crying as he pulled out his dick. See, he was the only man in her life that treated her with love and respect but after she did what she did, he lost all respect for her. He wasn't looking at it from her perspective, he was hurt so he wanted to hurt her back. And so he did. He treated her in a way he felt in the moment she needed to be treated, like a hoe. All she needed was love and guidance. They were both lost. This was really the first act of betrayal that broke me down. I already had low self-esteem but this incident and all the further occurring incidents continued to chip away at me. I was at work that evening. It was a school night; my mom picked me up from work. I was a sales rep at Addition Elle at the Trinity Mall location at the time. I went home, showered, got in my PJ's and called Lewis of course. It was our regular nightly routine. He sounded different this time though. Really somber and low toned. I knew something was wrong. He's like "I'm really sorry Stina." "For What?" I replied. "I met up with Sarah and tried to get her to give me head, but she didn't, she started crying and we left. I deleted her number and I'll never call or meet up with her again."

As I sat on the other end of the phone, my heart just sank into my chest. He gave me his word from when he was inside that he wasn't going to meet up with her. Although he didn't actually engage in the act with her, I felt so betrayed. That was the first real piece of my heart that was chiseled off. Of course I asked a million and one questions, did he kiss her, did she touch him, did she put her mouth on him, did he want to fuck her? I was asking total nonsense questions. I was trying to understand the extent and if he was lying. I remember him apologizing a million times and him saying he wouldn't do it again. As you can imagine I pretty much cried myself to sleep that night and a few nights to come. I didn't break up with him because I felt he was remorseful for the most part. I never dealt with the betrayal or the feeling it embedded within me. I just pushed past it, let it go. Let me tell you though, now looking back on everything that happened, every time I was hurt and cheated on, I never allowed myself to process the feelings in a healthy way. I cried about it, and buried it as many of us do. I believed all the "sorry baby, I won't do it again." It became so repetitive and I allowed it. For those reading this right now, please remember this, your partner will only do to you what you allow them to do to you! I allowed it by not setting consequences. I allowed it by showing Lewis that I wasn't going anywhere and I wasn't going to hold him accountable, there were no consequences. I was just going to cry and become more insecure about myself embedding it in my head that there was something wrong with me. That's what infidelity does to us, makes us feel we're not enough.

The Day I Became A Woman....

Some weeks passed after the whole Sarah incident. Things seemed back to normal, we were at his sister's apartment on Shoreham which is North Jane Street. Close to Steeles Ave. We hung out a bit, ate some food. OMG his big sis Leslie could throw down in the kitchen. Throw down means she could really cook. Her food was finger lickin' good, very rich but soooo good. I learned a little something from her in the kitchen over the years. So, we're there, just chilling and I see Lewis go and talk to his sister in the kitchen. I heard her make a comment, they're Trini so of course with a thick accent, She said, "okay I'll give you a bly" My heart started pounding when I saw her packing up the kids and leaving. Bly in Caribbean slang means: to give a break. I was about to be left entirely alone with Lewis in a private place for the first time ever. I went into that bathroom so quickly and locked the door. I just stood behind the door listening to everyone leave until I heard nothing at all. I stood there standing so still, staring in the mirror at myself. My breathing became incredibly shallow as my heart started to slow down.

I was trying to prevent a panic attack. Was this going to be the moment? The moment I lose my virginity? It was only February 11th 2004, He has only been out a little over a month, I want to wait at least until May 22nd, my 19th birthday. He knew this. Maybe we were just going to fool around a little, maybe just some hand play, he had to be back at the halfway house to sign in in just under 2 hours and we had to take a few buses to get back there. So I know there definitely wasn't enough time to go the full mile. He'd be late. After convincing myself that I'm good and I probably wasn't going to pop my cherry, I hear a knock at the bathroom door. Well don't I do a hop skip and a jump out of fright. My heart rate bounced right back up again, and I'm pretty sure now I started to buss a sweat out of anxiousness. (buss a sweat – start sweating)

"You good? How long are you going to be in there?" Lewis said with a smirk on his face. I could hear him smirking from the other side of the door. I wanted to say, I'll come out when your sister and her kids come back but I couldn't do that could I? Could I? I mean I could have. "I'll be out in a minute," I said in a timid tone. Would you believe this man tried to open the door? Oh Lord thank God I locked it. I told him again that I'd be out in a minute. I swear I wasn't in there for long but maybe I was and I wasn't paying attention. I finally opened the door and there he was, right there waiting for me with this passionate look in his eyes. Here we go. He came at me like a lion waiting to devour its prey. He gripped my waist, my ass, started touching me in places I've never been touched, started kissing me so passionately while leading me toward Leslie's bedroom. He made up the bed with fresh sheets and all. He gripped the bottom of my shirt and pulled it over my head. I've never shown a man even my upper body. I felt so exposed and vulnerable but I allowed it to continue. He laid me down on the bed, while kissing me, and slid his hand down my pants and started to play with my clitoris. He took his other hand and slid each strap of my bra down and exposed my breasts. His lips slowly made their way down my neck and to my chest as my breasts became the playground for his wandering tongue. Everything was happening so fast, I didn't want to go all the way but this feeling felt so good. The feeling was euphoric. I started thinking maybe if I give him me he won't cheat because he'll be getting sex from me. I'd have to get the hang of things and by what I was experiencing I think I'd love to get the hang of things quickly because I definitely wanted more of this. Before I knew it I was completely naked, I didn't even realize he had slid off my pants and undone my bra in the back. I covered up with a sheet as I didn't want him to see me naked. I didn't feel ready. He leaned over me and said, " stop hiding, let me see you." I lifted the sheet off a little bit and he looked at me with so much passion. I looked down and saw his hard at attention dick. I started freaking out because I knew this shit was about to hurt like nothing I've ever experienced before. He wasn't small at all if you know what I mean. Tampons hurt me, how in the world was I going to go through with this? He slid a condom on and started to proceed toward me. I knew I wasn't ready, I didn't want it to happen like this, in his sister's bed, barely no foreplay or exploring, and I was still 18! I envisioned the romantic settings we had spoken about, a dim room lit with candles, rose petals all over the place, wine, etc. I wanted it to be special because I knew what I had was special. No one had ever gotten this from me. Nevertheless, I gave in. I knew I loved him and we planned our future together. He tried to enter me a few times and it wasn't working. Maybe he just lost his technique after being locked up. I opened my legs a little wider as he tried again, this time I felt it. I screamed in pain as he tried to move too fast, he stopped immediately and asked if I was okay. I told him, "yes, please just go slow." He started to push again. The pain was horrible. It felt like someone was burning me with fire while tearing my skin. I can't believe this was happening, I was no longer a virgin. It was not enjoyable for me at all but I saw the passion and pleasure on Lewis' face as he slowly entered and exited me repeatedly. It was only a few minutes but it felt like forever. I wanted it to end. He finally came as I watched his face twitch in ways I've never seen before. He pulled himself out and looked down. He stood up and said, "there's no blood.". I was stunned because that sure as hell felt like I'd be torn apart down there. He seemed like he didn't believe that I was a virgin. He went to the bathroom, came back in the room with another condom on and entered me again. This time it wasn't slow and easy at all. He fucked me. I couldn't understand why he was doing that. I mean I was screaming before when he barely moved and now he was fucking me like I'd been having sex before him. I started crying and screaming as I laid there praying this would end. This time he lasted longer than just a couple minutes. It was more like 5 or so. He came again. He got up and looked at the time and realized we had to go back to the halfway house to sign in. He left the bedroom and closed the door. I got up and sat on the end of the bed in shock. What the hell just happened? Why did I let this happen? My virginity was just taken and wasn't even appreciated? Lewis came into the room and saw me still sitting there with the sheet wrapped around me. He looked at me and said, "yo yo, get up, get up, you're bleeding everywhere." I stood up quickly. I was in so much pain and disbelief I didn't even realize I was bleeding all over his sister's bed, her floor, and now that I was standing up the blood started leaking down my leg. I grabbed my clothes and rushed to the bathroom before I bled even more. I sat over the toilet and let the blood drip into the toilet bowl as I heard Lewis on the other end of the door trying to get the stains out of the mattress and changing the sheets. He called his sister and explained to her what happened and surprisingly she was cool. I was so embarrassed because I actually bled a lot. I mean who wouldn't after being fucked like that? His whole energy changed once he saw the blood and he was proud that his family got to see the stains as well. So none of them could say I wasn't a pure girl when he got with me. I got myself cleaned up, rolled up some toilet paper to catch any excess blood while on the bus ride, got dressed and put together enough to now hop on the bus to go back. I was in so much pain, I felt emotionally numb on the whole ride back. Lewis was happy, he was holding my hand, resting his arm over my shoulder as we rode the transit, and told me how much he loved me. I knew I loved him too. It's okay, I didn't get my dream moment; it happens I guess. We'll have plenty of other chances to make it what I had envisioned in my mind. But as for that day; that day I became a woman.

After that day we were really inseparable. We were intimate whenever we got the chance. I don't know what came over me. I was always a super reserved person but I wanted it any and everywhere. I became very experimental in terms of places we would have sex. I'm talking about stairwells, peoples apartments, high park in the dead of winter, the halfway house (multiple times). That was so exciting. We had sex on the parole officers desk, as the offices were under construction so they were accessible. The halfway house library, right there on the couch while the officers were on the other side of the door, movie theaters, etc. If we were in the mood it was on sight. I started to feel a little more confident that he wasn't going to cheat at all now. We were extremely compatible and in love. Things were going well, we both had jobs, he was attending programming, his time in the halfway house was counting down, we were looking for places, he had a decent job at UPS on Steeles. Everything was great, but I wasn't watching the signs. We weren't really communicating on a deep level, we were just existing and if there's another piece of advice I can leave you as the reader with, it would be to dig deep conversational wise and keep digging deep. Once we started having sex, our communication became almost surface level. Instead of taking time to talk we were looking for places to get busy. He started spiraling and I never knew. I wasn't paying attention. I blamed myself for a lot of it because I have always been the one who expresses a lot. I'm also one who has been born with a great gift, people of all walks of life, even people I just meet pour out their deepest darkest secrets to me without hesitation. I never knew what it was about me back then but I know now. I'm an Empath. Empaths are rare individuals with a God given ability to sense and feel things on a very deep level. I feel the pain of others and not only that, my energy screams I'm a safe space and people always feel safe with me. I'm a healer and people sense that and gravitate to me. Most times we get very overwhelmed as we take on everyone's energy, good or bad. I wish I could have really recognized and acted on the signs but I guess I was too young to really understand what was really going on. It was my first real relationship and on top of that I never even considered the traumas that he had to deal with during lock up. Young offender was no joke.

Despite him continuing to battle his undiagnosed mental health issues he tried his best wherever he could and I really appreciated that. Lewis is a man of action and that's how he shows his love. He planned the cutest surprise party for my 19th birthday. He called all my friends, rented a party room in The White Knight Motel on the corner of Dixie Rd and Derry in Mississauga. He stayed up all night making Kurma. He made way too much of it, like 4 whole trays too much, as a snack for everyone. Kurma is a hard sweet deep fried crunchy type of desert from Trinidad. It was the thought that counted though. He got my friends from Malton to DJ, my girls from my school etc. It was a vibe. I was a little drunk though so I don't remember a ton. That was the first time I had ever had someone plan a surprise party for me. I knew he loved me because he had never put effort into anyone like that in his life.

I went to see him one day when he was by his other sister's place at Keele and Sheppard. 3800 Keele to be exact and he was so intoxicated. They were having a party and I didn't want to interrupt it but I needed to tell him something in person. See I had just found out that I was actually pregnant and I had miscarried. I wasn't far along but I was emotional about it because I was on birth control the whole time. I felt like that's why the pregnancy didn't take, because I kept taking the pills.

I showed up and asked Lewis if we could speak in the stairwell privately. He was just trying to have sex, feeling me up, kissing me etc, but I had to tell him. "I just had a miscarriage," I blurted out. Now looking back of course I recognize that was horrible timing. This man is starting to spiral, he has unhealed traumas, he's intoxicated and now I'm throwing this at him? I felt horribly selfish for years after that because I felt like I was the one who made him spiral even more. But I was young, in my emotions, I had no one but him that I felt comfortable with to confide in. Plus, it's his child, he's my man, so why shouldn't I run to him when I need support and comfort? Only makes sense right? Wrong! He was taken back, stood there silent for a few moments, and consoled me as I started to cry. He embraced me like never before. I felt safe and acknowledged. We spent some time talking and I went home and he went back to the party. I thought we were okay, all was good until that phone call the next morning. Again, that familiar low somber voice that I had heard before penetrated my eardrum from the other end of the receiver. That tone eventually became the telltale sign that something bad had happened that would again chisel off yet another piece of my heart.

"I'm sorry" comes through. "What's wrong?" I responded. "I slept with someone last night."

I couldn't believe what I was hearing. I just had a miscarriage, I just recently gave myself to him in ways no one has ever had me, and this is what he does? I started crying like I never have in my life. Any confidence I had gained was destroyed by that one moment. Not only that, this moment here was the beginning of very skewed and unhealthy thought patterns that started to arise within my head. I started blaming myself for telling him about the things I was going through. For years I blamed myself for him becoming incarcerated again. I told myself that it was my fault for putting too much pressure on him. I should have known he couldn't handle it. After he got locked up the second time I started to shut down emotionally. I knew if I expressed myself it would end up in disaster so I held it all. But you know when you hold shit in it festers and grows into something much more horrific later on in life. We'll get into that later though. I want to make it very clear that I now know that it was never my fault for expressing how I felt. Yes, there could have been better times, I should have sought help but I know it is not my fault for his choices, nor is he at fault for my choices. We are all individuals and we all have our own free will and the ability to make our own decisions based on the circumstances. So please for those reading these words, know it is not your fault! It's one thing to take accountability for our actions but to blame ourselves for someone else's decision is wrong and very heavy on the soul.

I started to become someone I wasn't. Calling, texting, questioning everything, even showing up when I wasn't supposed to. I remember this one time I showed up unexpectedly to his middle sister's apartment. She lived at Jane and Wolner. Her and I don't really get along. I don't hate anyone as I have nothing but love in my heart for everyone but that's one person I will never forgive. She violated me and both of my kids horribly, and put my life and my childrens lives in danger on multiple occasions. When I come out with what happened in part two of my trilogy you'll completely understand why. Yes, my story has so many intricate parts that it needs to be written in three parts. I have way too much to cover. Anyway, who told me to show up unexpectedly on this particular weekend? He was set to party all weekend. He got a weekend pass and was going to take full advantage of it without me. I really should have respected his space but I didn't know how to act. I was an insecure mess. I went there early before he showed up. He walked in the door and had a shocked look on his face. Like I was interrupting his vibe, which I probably was. He asked me what I was doing here and I told him I wanted to surprise him. He knew it was bullshit. He knew I came because I didn't want him to have a whole weekend to himself to do what he wanted to do. I felt like I needed to keep tabs on him but what I was doing was making him feel like he was in prison again. He wanted to be free and I was incarcerating him again in a whole different way. I had brought some alcohol, blue Alize and vodka to be exact. We started drinking, we ate some food and later he told me he's going out and I'm not coming with him. That made me feel really fucked up but I did it to myself. I should have just stayed home and let him have his fun. I really had nothing to do other than to watch T.V. or talk on the phone. I waited for hours.

Finally I got fed up around 1 am and went out. There was a pizza shop that was open late right on the corner of Jane and Wolner. I bought a slice and just sat outside the shop chilling. Of course I was calling down his phone like a desperate girl, but I felt like I was. I wanted my man. I didn't want him to cheat again and again. Crazy thing is I thought I could stop him. A man's going to do what he wants to do. I stayed on the street for about an hour or so waiting to see if I saw him coming from either direction, or coming off the bus like a stalker. I got bored with nothing to do so I just went back to the apartment. He eventually came in around 2:30 am. Drunk and high but happy. He got undressed, ate some food and we immediately got right into it. No words exchanged or anything. We took it to the balcony, he told me to hold on to the balcony railing and bend over. We were completely naked out there having sex in front of the world like it's nobody's business. It was exciting, exhilarating, liberating almost. He came and told me to hold on a minute. Thought he was going to clean up, come back and get into it again. I remember it was cold and I was butt naked. After a few minutes I really started to feel it and Lewis wasn't back yet. I went to open the door and it was locked. I was thinking shit I didn't want to knock because everyone was sleeping. I peeked through the window and I saw Lewis sitting on the couch. I tapped the window and he just looked at me. I told him to open the door and I was locked out. He just ignored me. I was so confused. Why the fuck would you leave me naked on the balcony in the cold for? This man left me out there for a while. I had no way to get back in. I curled up in the corner to try to keep myself warm until he opened the door. He finally unlocked it and let me in. We said nothing to one another; I passed him and went into the bathroom. I started sobbing uncontrollably as I got into the shower. I finished up, got dressed and went to sleep on the couch. I really should have gone home at that point but I loved him and saw the beautiful person behind all the B.S. The next day we spent the day together like any normal day and I went home in the evening. He did apologize later for his behavior. See now I don't want you to judge him for that. Yes it was not acceptable but this is clearly a response to trauma. Lewis was and is still an extremely loving and caring person. He has great characteristics, he's a great dad, but he needed help and I wasn't helping. I was adding to the stressors. He thought, in that moment, he was teaching me a lesson to not show up unexpectedly again which of course Christina and her stubborn nature did do it again, but the outcome wasn't as bad. He had been abused all his life, that's all he knew. When you don't know anything else, how can you do better? I was hurt and still am hurt by it because things like that you don't forget, but I moved on. Time passed, the cycle continued, but for the most part things started getting better. Lewis became more focused, he got his own little place off Marley Ave and even though there was just one chair and a twin mattress on the floor I was there with him the first night he spent there. We shared that little twin mattress, made love on that twin mattress, sat and talked, ate, everything on that twin mattress. That was love 'cause I'm a big girl so you can imagine how hard that was to share a bed that size with another full sized human being. He only stayed there about one month before he got arrested again. York Regional Police called one day asking him to turn himself in for some alleged theft at his UPS workplace. Some T.V.s were sent to his sister's address and she immediately pointed them in his direction. I didn't know what was going to happen that day but I was preparing myself for him to be locked up again. I didn't know how the law worked, I just thought that because he had done time for a serious crime before that he was going to do time again. My mom was the one who dropped him to the Police station in Vaughan. I held onto him so tight while crying. We kissed and he left my arms. We waited and prayed for hours to see what was happening. I swear my heart skipped a beat every time I saw that door opening, hoping it would be him that would walk out. Just as we were about to start talking about heading home the door opened one last time. It was Lewis. Oh my God my heart leapt out of my chest. I ran out to hug him. He got a promise to appear! A promise to appear is you being let out on your own recognizance; where they hold you responsible to show up to your scheduled court dates.

We decided that now he was fired from his job he'd move to Brampton to be closer to me. I called my friend Cynthia and asked her if he could rent a room from her and she was cool with it. So we headed to Brampton where he'd remain until he got arrested for first degree murder, which is the sentence, he's serving time for now. I was so happy, I was going to find him a job, he'd be so close to me, I could sleep over whenever I wanted to and we'd really get to start our life together. We spent the first night together at Cynthia's place.

Shortly after he moved to Brampton I had a weird premonition, I wasn't pregnant at this time but I dreamt I was holding a newborn baby boy as I stared at him through thick paned glass in his bright orange jail jumpsuit. I told him about this but he never took it seriously and neither did I. It was so early in our journey I think we both forgot. I remember this one-day in particular where my mom was freaking out on me for having her car all the time and she was threatening me saying that if I didn't bring the car back home, or sleep at home that night that I could never come back to the house again. I told Lewis I couldn't spend the night with him this time but he started crying. I couldn't understand why and neither could he. He just said he needed me to stay and he didn't want to be alone but I was placed in a horrible position between him and my mom. I stayed as long as I could but I eventually left. That was a mistake. I should have stayed because that's where everything started to go downhill when it came to his emotions. He needed me and I didn't come through. That moment reminded me of that one moment in *Love and Basketball* where Q wanted Monica to stay with him after he found out about his dad's infidelities and she was more concerned about her curfew and starter position in the game. Everything was seemingly fine for some time but then everything went downhill after that and that is exactly what I feel happened.

Some time passed and we moved to Cynthias' new place and Lewis took over the basement. We now had our own full space. We started furnishing the basement and creating a nice little comfy place to call home. I still lived at home with my parents but I stayed over with Lewis quite frequently at this point. Lewis found a great job as a gas marketer and really started bringing in the money. One day we were chilling and out of nowhere I got nauseous. I barely made it to the toilet in time. The next day I decided to go grab one of those sticks ya pee on and guess what? Yup you guessed it, it came back positive! I was pregnant. I remember I showed Lewis the positive pregnancy test in the middle of the North Gate Plaza parking lot during an argument. I don't remember what we were arguing about but it was one of those "Oh yeah, by the way I'm pregnant," type of statements to shut him up. He looked at the test in surprise and smiled. "Don't act all surprised" I Said, "You know you were trying to get me pregnant that day." Lewis just kept smiling and told me to get in the car so we could go home.

The doctors' appointments started, he was happy, I was happy, we were happy. Things were starting to finally normalize again.

He was working crazy long hours at work. He'd wake up at 5:30 am and wouldn't get home until 10pm or 11pm and have to do it all over again the next day. He wasn't eating or sleeping properly. The not eating properly part was on me. As his woman I feel I should have been taking better care of him. Yes, I was working and going to school as well but I had more time than he did so I should have been cooking meals for him. I didn't really know how to cook Caribbean dishes back then and that's all he would eat. He didn't complain but he did tell me he wanted his big sister and mom to teach me how to cook. Of course I agreed because I do love to cook, I just cooked European style foods at that point. We were doing okay but then something happened where he started cheating again and I was pregnant. I really didn't want to put myself at risk like that. We eventually decided when I was about 5 months pregnant to take a break, a real break this time. Like a no communication type of break. I was almost 5 months at this point. I remember going for the ultrasound alone and getting 2 copies of the sonogram pics. That's the day I found out we were having a baby boy. I called Lewis to share the excitement but he didn't answer. So I went by the house and put the pic in the side door mailbox where he could get it when he came home. I texted him to let him know it was there but no response. The next morning Cynthia calls me and tells me to get to the house right away. I was half asleep because it was like 7am on a Saturday morning. She yelled at me, "wake your ass up and get over here, I got the bitches shoes!" What type of drugs are you on girl is really what I wanted to say to her but then she said it again, "Lewis has a bitch downstairs and she can't leave because I have the bitches shoes. Get your ass over here now!" I heard her loud and clear that time. I hopped up out of bed, took my moms keys and flew over there. I went through the upstairs door and sat down and spoke to Cynthia for a bit so we could formulate a plan. In reality I had no business being there. We were on a break, he could fuck who he wanted, he had a free pass but I was pregnant, hormonal and emotional so I acted out. Plus we had this unhealthy type of possessive love over one another. It's like we owned one another. I finally decided to just go downstairs and sit on the couch outside his bedroom door. He really had another woman in our bed. Crazy thing is I also had a premonition about this exact same scenario when he was still locked up. I told him, I keep having this recurring dream where I catch you with another woman in our bed. He reassured me that would never happen because he was a one-burner man and he would never disrespect our bed in such a way. Welp, tadaaaaaa. It happened! So I sat there for a while, I listened as they started to get back into it. Or maybe that was in my head. I swear I heard some type of noises. I knocked on the door and Lewis opened it. The look on his face was priceless. He looked like he just saw a ghost. I just looked at him in disgust at this point and said, "in our bed?" I sat back on the couch, Cynthia and her kids came down and by no means was that a situation for a child to witness so I did tell them to go back upstairs. They just wanted to make sure I was okay because I did start to get hysterical at one point. She finally came out and said she's sorry and she didn't know he was with anyone. She then proceeded to say they didn't do anything. Haha yeah okay, sure buddy. Like I believed that. She eventually left so Lewis and I could talk. We spoke about what we were going to do, decided we'll still remain on a break until we work things out. I asked him if I had permission to go seek someone else just because I wanted to see what he was going to say. Of course he said no. I was still his according to him. We didn't speak for a few weeks after that unless it was about the baby and even those conversations were minimal because we really weren't planning; we were just taking it day by day. After a lot of conversations and Lewis realizing that his family is what he really wants we gave it another shot.

The Engagement

I woke up early on a Saturday morning as the sun beamed in on our face from the large basement window. We were positioned face to face as I smiled at him sleeping while holding my growing belly. I was about six months pregnant at the time, maybe close to seven. I stared at him for about five minutes before he opened his eyes and smiled at me. He outstretched his arms and pulled me in close, kissed me on my forehead and told me how much he loved me. He rubbed my belly and then started to kiss me passionately. One thing led to another and we made the most passionate love that morning. The energy was just right, he had the weekend off so he didn't have to rush off to work early in the morning. We were able to just enjoy one another's presence for a change. We eventually got up, showered and got ready. He said he was taking me to his sister's house because he planned a baby shower for me. I was so excited, I was about to be spoiled. We showed up and all his family were there, some of my friends, friends of friends, and a ton of food. And you know a pregnant girl gotta eat so I was happy about that. We ate, listened to music, laughed, etc. It was a great day. I do remember a friend of his family making a rude comment about me, Lewis escorting her out of the apartment in front of everyone. I don't remember what she said but clearly it was disrespectful enough to have him embarrass her like that. I felt protected at that moment. Like yeah, my man went to bat for me, he stood up for me. That moment I fell more in love with him. I had an amazing time. The night came to an end, everyone left, we packed up, cleaned up and headed home. I drove home because he was a little intoxicated and of course I'm automatically the DD (designated driver) due to pregnancy.

While on the way home we were talking about marriage and where we saw ourselves in the near future. I told him, "I need a beautiful diamond ring first, just saying." We both laughed.

He smiled, leaned over and then pulled a small box out of his back pocket. I started to shake. "No you didn't, no it's not."

A Story of a Prison Wife

He opened the box and there sat a beautiful Birks Gold Band with a flower diamond shape inset. It was so cute. I had to pull over because I was swerving into the next lane trying to catch a good glimpse. He closed the box and put it back in his pocket. I was all smiles, he said let's go home and you can look at it there. As I continued to drive, he mentioned that he wanted to propose in front of everyone but that one person salted up the whole vibe. I totally understood. Lewis was a "vibes" type of person. If the vibe isn't right, he follows his gut. We arrived home, he opened the door for me, brought in all the food as I sat on the couch waiting for him. He stood in front of me just staring at me smiling. He got down on bended knee, opened the box to present it to me properly, and asked me to marry him.

"Stina, will you be my wife?"

Of course I said yes!!! I started crying, I always cry by the way. Anyone who knows me knows I'm a crybaby. I cry for every damn thing!

What happened next was hilarious. He takes this beautiful ring out of the box and attempts to place it on my ring finger...... Well, first let me say I do not and never did have big fingers. I think my fingers are average sized. Maybe I'm biased but I'm sure I have cute hands. Why does this man attempt, yes I say attempt... to put the ring on my finger and it didn't even reach the first finger joint or knuckle. He let out this embarrassed laugh and I started laughing as well. I was like damn I wanted to wear the ring.

"You couldn't have snuck my ring size or anything?" I asked while laughing. He shook his head and told me he's sorry. I was so okay, it was funny, I just wanted to give him a little bit of a hard time by cracking some jokes on him. We kissed and made love again right there on the living room floor. The next day we made it a priority to resize the ring. It only cost him $50 at this one jeweler we stopped at off of Steeles, close to Jane.

After we got it resized, he placed it on my finger and let me tell you, it fit beautifully! We were officially engaged! Maybe now everything will be okay moving forward?

Shortly thereafter, let's say about a few weeks, we had a falling out with Cynthia because she was going downstairs and stealing Lewis's weed from his weed drawer. We decided it was time to move. I found this cute little 1 bedroom apartment on Larkspur in Brampton. It was only $650 per month. Done and done, we took it, and didn't even have to sign a lease. We moved our stuff in and that was it. We seemed to have another period of stability up until I was about seven and a half to eight months pregnant. Yet another cheating situation arose, this time it was his sister that ratted him out. I was taking a nap in my room at my moms house when my phone rang. It was Lewis' sister, the middle one who I don't get along with. I hear her voice and then she clicks her line over. I hear another woman's voice on the other end of the line. She says Christina, Lewis is cheating on you. This is his next woman Karen. Karen, meet Lewis' wife. She said hello, I said hello, and it just so happened that Lewis was there with her.

She told him that his wife was on the phone, he immediately grabbed the line and said hello. I replied, "Hi Lewis." He started cussing and getting on all kinds of ways and hung up the phone. I thanked his sister and hung up. A few minutes later he started ringing off my cell phone. I was not going to answer at all. I was trying to protect my peace at that point. Well doesn't he start ringing off my house phone.

I told my mom I didn't want to talk to him at all but she eventually convinced me to talk to him.

"What do you want, Lewis?"

He profusely apologized yet again but to be very honest at this point I was just exhausted. I was about to give birth in about a month or so and I was just tired. I was still working too, overnights to boot so I needed to rest. We decided that we were going to take another break from our relationship and I agreed. I was tired of fighting for someone who didn't want to fight for me. I was celibate from that day to the time we had our first trailer visit when our son was almost 3 years old. My maternity leave started and I started prepping for the baby. Getting all the baby clothes in order, car seat, playpen, diapers, formula, etc.

Lewis and I spoke but not like we did before. It was weird, we were having a baby with one another but we were strangers. I can't describe how alone I felt in those moments. I had no one to really console me and support me in the way I needed it. I needed my man, my child's father, my future husband. My friends were around, my mom was around but after witnessing everything happen, how it happened, and what toll it took on me. I don't think anyone knew how to really support me. Plus I was always the person who put on this strong persona like I can handle anything life threw at me, I would never ask for help even when I needed it. That became one of my most toxic traits that I still battle with til' this day. I'd give anyone the shirt off of my back but when it came to me asking for help I couldn't do it. I do remember spending the most memorable moments with my dad during the end of my pregnancy. I'd sit in the living room with him and we'd watch all the oldie shows I watched with him as a child growing up. He never asked me about how I was feeling mentally, I think he knew, he must have heard me crying in my room every night. Those walls were paper-thin. I knew it hurt him to see me like this. I was his only child, and a daughter at that. Despite my upbringing we started to become closer as I got older. He drank less and started to enjoy life a little more. He was about to be a grandpa.

The Birth Of A New Life…..

I had everything prepped and set up in our little basement apartment that no one really ever went to, and I was about ready to give birth. My original due date was the end of July. I had my follow-up appointment around August 1st or so and that's when they told me they were going to probably have to induce me. I decided rather than having them chemically induce me I would take a tablespoon of castor oil to naturally induce my labour. I did a ton of research and realized it was the option for me. After dinner on August the 4th 2005, I took it, and let me tell you, it was the nastiest thing I've ever tasted in my life. The texture made me shiver and shake. It was so gross. It's 10 times worse than Buckleys. I told my dad that I was going upstairs to take a nap and off I went. I watched T.V. in my room for a bit before I fell asleep. I woke up around midnight or so with the most horrible cramps. Castor oil also helps clear your bowels so that's really all it was. I had to really go to the bathroom. After that I went back to sleep until about 2 hours later. Cramps again but this time it was different. I ran to the bathroom and before you know it my water broke. I hopped in the bathtub and called for my mom. "mom, MOOOM!," "yeahhhh," she replied.

"I think my water broke."

"Okay, let's get ready to go to the hospital, I'll be in the car waiting for you."

I took a quick shower, grabbed my diaper bag and everything I needed and off we went. The entire time I was trying to call Lewis but his phone was off. I kept calling for hours, even after I checked in at the hospital I wasn't getting a hold of him. Finally I decided to call one of his friend's numbers that he called me from once. I had great timing because they were actually together at that exact time. I told him I was in labor, to hurry up and get to the hospital. He showed up about an hour later ready for the world. We were both happy he made it because I wasn't about to bring this baby into the world alone. I needed him there.

We both discussed that I didn't want to take the epidural but that pain was starting to kick in. To the men reading this, I'm sure you know this already, but us women really have to endure a lot and that child-birthing labour pain is like nothing else you will have to experience. Women are Goddesses and deserve to be treated as nothing less than that. Period!

I was only about 4 or 5 cm dilated at that point and I was ready to take the needle. Lewis kept encouraging me, "Stina, remember what you said you wanted, no epidural."

He was right, we walked around the halls, he helped me to the bathroom, he sat beside me when I was in the large tub filled with water while rubbing my back and belly. He was so supportive and exactly what I needed in those moments. I started to fall in love with him all over again. This is the Lewis I knew. The loving, caring, supportive, take charge man.

After about 11 or 12 hours of labour I told him I needed the epidural. I was sitting on the edge of the bed having the worst contractions while holding onto him crying out for the epidural. He kept trying to steer me away from it but I gave in. I couldn't do it anymore. Lewis supported me through the entire process. Once I got the Epidural I was able to knock right out. We both got some well-needed rest.

Before I knew it, I was 10cm dilated and ready to bring this little man into the world. Lewis was holding my hand the entire time and telling me to push. I still remember the excitement in his eyes until today. If there's one thing I knew for sure, it was that Lewis was going to be an amazing father. He loved kids and basically raised a few of his nieces and nephews when he was young. One last push and Mr. I.J. was born into this world. They placed him on my chest, I wiped him down and held my baby boy for the first time. That child saved my life, is the reason why I'm still here today. Lewis cut the umbilical cord and just stood there smiling at us.

The nurses took him, checked his weight, clamped his cord, cleaned him and wrapped him up. Lewis immediately took him, sat down and got lost staring at him.

My mom told us she was going home and that she'll leave us to talk. We never did though, we just enjoyed the moment, the moment we officially became a family of 3.

Healing after the birth is a whole chore. That's a whole different pain that no one really talks about but it wasn't fun.

Especially going to the bathroom. Sorry, is that TMI? Let's stay on track shall we?

In the days we were released and allowed to go home Lewis was really the one who showed me how to take care of a baby. Prior to this I had never changed, bathed or fed a newborn baby. He showed me how to bathe him for the first time. I remember watching him in awe holding this tiny, little, mini him in his large hand. Showing me how and where to wash, how to avoid the belly button area and keep it dry. He let me know it would fall off in about a week and his belly button would start to form. Need I say more? He literally taught me everything about caring for a newborn. He spent a couple days with me at home until I got the hang of caring for our son on my own. Then he went back to work. And by "back to work" I mean, "back to hustling" but I didn't know then. I thought he had a job at the time but he was selling drugs. A couple weeks passed and everything was great. We were cohabitating well, we were communicating without arguing, he was spending more nights at home, helping me with the baby. We weren't together but we were okay.

The Day Our Lives Changed Forever

September 1, 2005 was like any other day. I.J. was now 28 days old and Lewis was home from work. The only thing that was weird was the landlord upstairs told us that the cable man was here to check the connection and needed to come downstairs. It seemed odd because he was staring at Lewis the entire time and watching his movements. After the cable guy left, Lewis told me he was going to walk to the corner store to grab some snacks. About forty minutes later I came to hear a heavy knock at the door. It seemed odd because Lewis wouldn't knock so heavily knowing his son is sleeping. Maybe he had forgotten his keys so I opened the door. To my surprise, it wasn't Lewis. There were two strange men standing at my basement door. I was terrified because you have to have a key to enter through the garage door to get to my basement entrance. They showed me their badges, identified themselves as police officers and told me I had to come down to the police station with them. They explained that Lewis had just been arrested and they needed to speak

Police Station where I was brought for interrogation

A Story of a Prison Wife

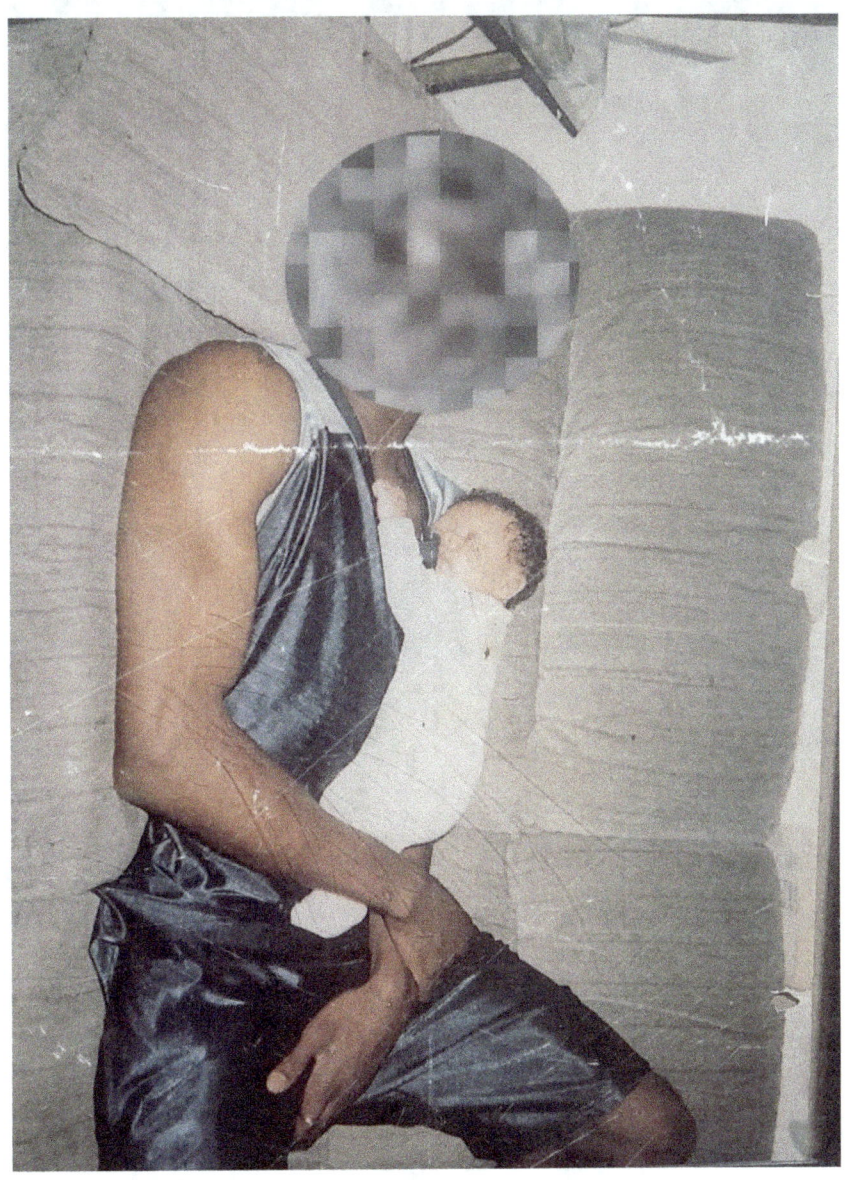

The last time father and son were together on the outside

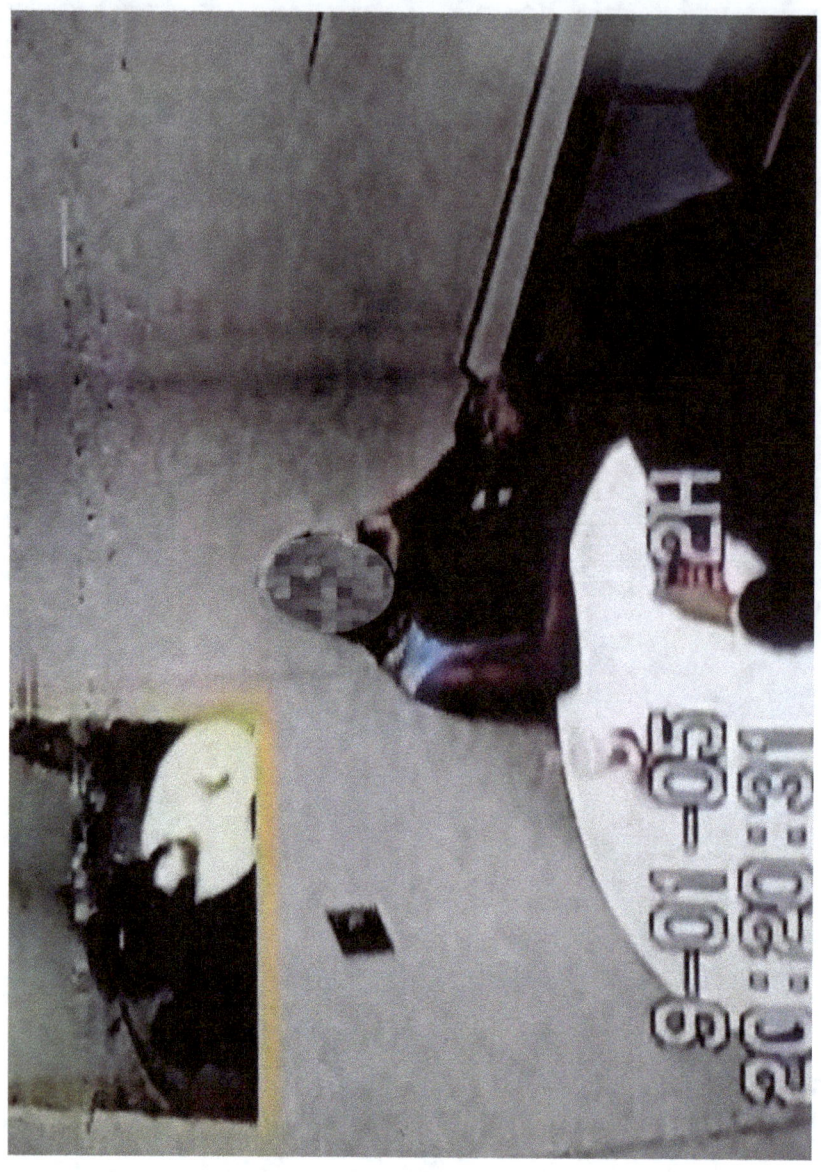

Just hours later facing a first degree murder charge.

with me immediately. They wouldn't tell me what they arrested him for. They also said; And I quote, " because you are not the accused or a victim, you have no rights and you have to come with us." They were wrong; they were lying. Here I was to be a victim of their many wrong doings. I told them that I have a 28-day-old child and I was very tired due to being up all night with the baby. The Sergeant in charge didn't care and said I have to bring the baby.

Being scared, exhausted, and completely naïve, I went with them. I didn't know any better. I packed up the baby, car seat, a little formula, packed a diaper bag; enough for only a few hours, locked the door and got in their unmarked police car. They then told me they need my keys. I refused at first but they told me that they will be forced to knock down the door and I will be responsible for paying the landlord for all the damages incurred. I got scared because I had no money coming in. How was I supposed to pay for a damaged door? I was still waiting on my E.I. benefits to kick in and I that wasn't even going to be enough to live on let alone replace a door. So I gave them my keys not knowing they wouldn't let me go back into my house until after they got a search warrant and executed it.

When we were driving the one officer told me he had been charged for 1st degree murder. I couldn't believe my ears, I felt sick to my stomach, MURDER??? This had to be a mistake, This is someone who had just had a baby, who was there for his birth. Although we were going through our issues we were working on us, and we were still engaged. He was working like crazy for us, I had seen paychecks from Ontario energy in amounts from $500 to $2500 per week. We were doing okay. This had to be a mistake; this couldn't be. I cried most of the drive and then we pulled up to the homicide department on Derry Rd in Mississauga. I was panicking inside. I thought for sure this had to be a nightmare. They made me climb so many stairs. Baby in a car seat, holding a diaper bag, all while I was still in pain from the healing process from birth. He told me there wasn't an elevator. Damn liar! They sat me in a cold room and questioned me for hours. I was so exhausted from no sleep, from crying, etc. This couldn't be real. They questioned me about his associations, his whereabouts everyday, etcetera, I finally told him I wanted to go home and he said that's fine, he was done with me and he was satisfied that I was telling the truth. But, he said that I couldn't go back to our basement. He said that there may be evidence there and I have to find somewhere else to stay. They said a family member or hotel or a friend. First of all I had no money, I told him that all I had left was a few hundred dollars on the living room table in our apartment. I had no money in my account, only Lewis' account but his finances were seized now. They took our Land Rover for a search, so I had no transportation, I had no extra money to buy formula, diapers, clothes, wipes, nothing! Absolutely Nothing! Everything was in the apartment. I asked them what I should do because I had nothing and they said for me to ask some friends for help. I was already shocked at this whole ordeal and now they want me to tell everyone what happened. Assholes! I ended up staying in my mom's filthy house for almost a week. I had to clear out an area for us to live because, remember, my mom was and is still a severe hoarder. At this point I had no choice but to go home to moms. I stayed there in one clean area of the upper floor. After about six days I had to call the police department and ask them if I could have my truck back and they said my truck was ready for pickup 3 days ago. Why didn't they contact me to let me know so I could at least have transportation? They also said that I could get the keys to our basement as well. So I picked up the truck and of course it was ripped apart inside. They destroyed the wires that ran to the heated seats and the under seat cd deck. But nothing could compare to what I was about to witness when I got back home to our basement apartment.

A Story of a Prison Wife

THE AFTERMATH - Sept 9th 2005

I walked through the door, looked around and immediately dropped to my knees in tears. Everything in my sight was destroyed. Everything! Even the ceiling tiles were ripped down. All the couches were ripped open, my mattress was ripped open, the baby's mattress from his crib was cut open. The playpen and bassinet were destroyed. One of the glass tables was broken, my clothes and the baby's clothes were all over the floor with rotting food from the fridge and freezer all over them. Cereal and cookie containers dumped all over the place. Sugar bags poured out. Our clothes were destroyed. I had 3 large cans of powdered baby formula on the counter and those were dumped in the sink and in the garbage, some of our clothes were on the kitchen floor. Cereal, milk, sugar, juice, bananas, ground beef, fish, seasonings, fruits, vegetables, meats, cheese, etc were all left to rot. Who does this to a mother and child without any thought of what grief it would cause them? Who? It looked like I had just experienced a devastating tornado. Only the walls were standing. T.V. was broken, DVD and VCR player just thrown like trash, some of my CD's we cracked, scented candles that were once on my gorgeous glass tables were dug out, every last shampoo and body wash bottle was emptied in the bathroom. Every cleaning product, Tide, Mr. Clean, Lysol and bleach dumped. I walked for about 2 hours just staring at everything. I didn't know what to do or where to start. Everything we had invested in as parents was garbage now. I understood that the police had a job to do but why be so insensitive and destroy everything? Why dump out baby formula? Why rip apart the baby's mattress? Why throw rotting food on our clothes? This was all that I had! They clearly knew that there was a young baby but they still didn't care. They meant to take everything away from us. They were heartless at that moment and meant to hurt us. I was so distraught that I just sat on the floor crying for the next hour. I felt so alone, betrayed, and empty. At that moment it hit me that life, as I once knew it was over, there was to be no more happiness, comfort, security, and bliss. The living nightmare had just begun. This was the beginning of the turmoil and heartache I was going to experience.

I had to start all over again from nothing and with nothing. Then I remembered that I had over $300 on the glass table and I could at least buy a few baby items and formula so I looked for it and it wasn't there. I searched and searched for hours and found no money. Suddenly it dawned on me that the police took it. I called right away and asked for my money and they said "what money?" I got so mad; I told them while in the interrogation room, on camera, that I had money sitting right on the table.

$365 to be exact! They knew exactly what money I was talking about. I knew exactly how many bills I had in each denomination because I had just counted it. After a couple of hours, they called me back and said they had my money and that I could come pick it up. They tried to rob me after everything they had already done to us. The worst thing about all of this was that they didn't find anything they were looking for, NOTHING! They did all of this for no reason. They destroyed all of our belongings for no evidence whatsoever. The landlord was so upset and, understandably so, told me I had to vacate immediately. I mean his ceiling was on the floor for goodness sake. This home was his asset. I felt so embarrassed that this happened, everyone in the neighbourhood stared at me and ran inside when they saw me like I was some sort of criminal. So now here I was, 20 years old, I had a 35-day-old newborn, $365 in my pocket, nowhere to live, no one to turn to other than my parents, what was I going to do? What would you do in this situation? There I am back at my parents house in my old room. A smoke filled hoarder house, with a newborn baby and nothing to feed him or clothe him with. My mom ran to shoppers and grabbed what she could. A few bottles, some formula, a few little onesies, some pampers and wipes. Thank God he was a summer baby so it was still quite hot outside. I couldn't help but be furious with the police as they saw I had nothing. I had never developed such a deep hatred for them until then. Like we never fucked with police but after being treated that way with a newborn I understood everything. I understood the pain and fear communities felt when having to deal with these types of situations. It was disgusting. We are all human beings and for a human to treat another human being in such a manner was disgusting. Something inside me changed that day. So here I am in my old bedroom with just a few necessities to get by. I bathed my son, fed him and put him to sleep. I fell on the floor in a corner of my bedroom, curled up, sitting there looking at my baby boy sleeping on my bed so at peace. I just broke down like I never broke down before. That moment I realized this is it. It's just us. I felt so many emotions, I felt like life was over. A first-degree murder charge when we have a newborn baby???? Are you serious? I was also furious at him. I couldn't understand why someone would make that type of choice or put yourself around people that can jeopardize your freedom after starting a new family? I was so heartbroken and I felt abandoned with nowhere to turn. I cried out to God asking him why, why me, why my child? Why was I chosen to walk this path in life? I didn't understand then. I had no insight, no knowledge and very little life experience. I knew I was with a serious man, a fearless man ready for whatever but he was such a loving man. He had big dreams. I see the loving caring provider, the soft side. I ignored the signs of deep seeded trauma and pain for so long. I saw only what I wanted to see in the moments I wanted. I had to now face the rest of my life alone, raising a child on my own. I wasn't prepared for this at all.

Deep Seeded Pain

She sits under the dark sky wallowing in loneliness, wondering if it's true strength that she prays she'll one day possess. Because to her depression, sadness and tears is not strength, to her it resembles weakness, fears and the inability to overcome what seems easy for others to bear. But then she comes to the realization that not many can walk in her path. She's been torn down, abandoned, and ignored. Cheated and beaten with lies and tossed aside.

He's loyal to the game but she's loyal to him. Gave him her very innocence that was taken for granted. He was always willing to risk it all to be with one bitch for one night, on multiple nights. All while she's pregnant about to give birth to his first-born son. She tried to speak but he shut her down. She was being stabbed in the heart and head repeatedly with an energy that spread worthlessness and disgrace. This woman who gave him everything and asked for nothing in return ended up getting the worst part. Pregnant and alone, with no one to lean on she had to depend on herself. He was out there chasing the game and she's worried about how she's going to clothe his newborn son.

They say hell hath no fury like a woman scorned but this woman scorned hath no fury left. The fire had been put out. She lost it when she lost her desire to live. The only thing that kept her here in this world we live in was the young king she pushed out of her life giving womb. A New life arose in her when she set eyes on that piece of her. He brought warmth to her heart, ignited the fire of life and love again. He was her new life, he saved her life, and to him she is forever indebted, because without that little boy in her arms, she would have been dead…

Thank you!

I want to take a minute to sincerely thank you as the reader, as my supporter for sharing your most valuable asset you have in life with me, something we can never get back; your TIME! Thank you for taking your time to read the introduction to my story and I can only hope that my story has added some value and understanding in your life when it comes to someone in my situation. This was an extremely hard and frightening step to take but I knew I had to. Not only for myself and my healing journey but also for those families who are just like mine. My story is not one of a kind. It happens to many of us and I want to let these families know that they're not alone and they can and will make it through.

Although it's a grueling and tiresome journey you will make it through, that I promise you! Just keep fighting.

My never-ending fear has now turned into excitement for where this journey will bring me. Thank You so much again for taking this journey with me I am forever humbled at the opportunity to let you in.

"BEYOND FEAR IS FREEDOM"
LOVE CHRISSY

Chrissy . B.

www.ingramcontent.com/pod-product-compliance
Lightning Source LLC
Chambersburg PA
CBHW050248010526
44107CB00003B/233